Learn the New Rules of Money

Carl "Coach" Randolph
LEARN THE NEW RULES OF MONEY

Learn the New Rules of Money

The money game has changed.

Carl "Coach" Randolph
Forex/Crypto

Carl "Coach" Randolph
LEARN THE NEW RULES OF MONEY

@ 2019 Carl Randolph

All rights reserved. No part of this publication may be reproduced or distributed in any form or by any means, electronically or mechanically, including scanning, photocopying, recording, retrieval system or otherwise without prior written permission from the author, except for the inclusion of brief quotes in a review.

Cover design by Aaron Randolph
Houston, Texas

Edited by Gwen Hughes
Dallas, Texas

Published by Carl Randolph
Houston, Texas

Other books:
Http://HowToFindYourPassionAndGetWhatYouWant.com
Http://HowToMakeContactsAndWinFriends.com

Quantity discounts are available on bulk purchases of this book for educational or gift purposes.

Request for permission to make copies of any part of this workbook can be made at Cas@CoachRandolph.com.

Http://LearnTheNewRulesOfMoney.com

What are people saying about *Learn the New Rules of Money?*

This book is a great starter for those who are seeking more information outside of just searching around on the Internet about trading Forex. I've been trading for about two years now and I went through a pretty detailed academy, and this book is spot on with what you need to know on an introductory level. I feel this book will open your mind up to the possibility and give you enough information to make a decision on becoming a forex trader. This industry has absolutely impacted my family's life, and I hope that this book impacts your family as well. Thanks, Carl, for your rigorous research to always help others improve!

~Randy Webb Retired C-130 Pilot/Forex Trader

Carl Randolph's introduction into the world of Forex is a wake-up call of epic proportions. His honesty and insight truly inspired me to master this skill set that will pay me for a lifetime. This book is a great resource for a new person to learn the basics. Thank you, Coach Carl, for always being willing to share your knowledge with others!

~Dirk Leshan

Carl "Coach" Randolph
LEARN THE NEW RULES OF MONEY

Coach Carl presents a "How To" manual for the novice trader! With hands-on experience, Coach divulges the world's best-kept secret within the pages of this book. I implore you to dream bigger and commit to changing your mindset. Once you change your mindset, you will change your life.

~ReNita K. Antoine, J.D.

"*Learn the New Rules of Money* is a complete game changer. Coach Carl eloquently expresses the importance of generational wealth and financial freedom by utilizing the foreign exchange markets as a vehicle. His leadership and guidance throughout this learning process has been instrumental in helping me achieve success in the foreign exchange markets and in life!"

~Lindsi Thompson

Money matters! The Bible declares that the love of money is the root of all evil. I affirm this as truth. However, I have often declared in jest, "The lack of money will make you evil!" As a Senior Pastor in the well-known and maybe even notorious city of Compton in California, I have discovered that oftentimes it is the lack of knowledge and understanding concerning how money works that renders our people unable to generate a sustainable income, let alone create wealth. This book is excellently written and laid out by Carl "Coach" Randolph and helps bring clarity to how strategically and purposefully handling money in the Forex global market can create generational wealth!

**~Dr. Kevin E. Stafford, Senior Pastor
Zion Baptist Evangelistic Temple, Compton, CA**

Carl "Coach" Randolph
LEARN THE NEW RULES OF MONEY

Dedication

I dedicate this book to my five grandchildren who are the loves of my life. **Sinnead,** when I think of you, a big smile comes across my face. I am so proud of the young lady you have become. You are traveling around the world doing your own thing, and now you are an author. Big congratulations to you on your book, *Moody Nails, The Mudra Guidebook.* You keep being you and keep touching the lives of others.

Bianca, you are my free-spirited grandchild. You have no fear, and you let people know what's on your mind. There is no doubt in my mind that you are going to make a big impact in this world. You are going to touch so many lives, and I could not be prouder of you.

Gabriel, you just turned nine years old and, I have to admit (and not just because you are my grandson), you are one of the smartest nine-year olds I have ever known. You have a big heart and a loving spirit. You are such a giver, and full of energy. I know without a shadow of a doubt that you will inspire so many people to be better than they are.

Gideon, my strong-willed grandson, when you set your mind on something, you don't let go. I know whatever you decide to do with your life, you will be completely successful. At only six years old, you are much more mature than most others your age. You have a lot of knowledge for one so young, and I know you will use it wisely.

Carter, wow, oh wow! I cannot believe you are two years old already! It seems like you were just born. What a joy it has been watching you grow. Memaw has a few nicknames for you already: Busybody and Little Man, to name a couple. I can't wait to see what you become. I am sure whatever you want to be, you will become the best at it. Your big smile brings joy to my life every day.

Inspiration

A lot of people think inspiration comes from motivational speakers, **but true inspiration really comes from within.** You can be inspired in various ways: a good movie, pages from a book, a conversation with a friend, a sermon, or it could even come from a child. The question is, are you open to listening and not just hearing? I was inspired by two videos about Forex that changed my life forever, and I cannot thank the couple and the individual enough for posting them.

Keep your options open and be willing to listen to other people that you trust and admire. Take the information, break it down, and see if what they are talking about can help you. Some people tell me they hate what they are doing, they don't like their job, or they don't make enough money. What gets me is when I offer other options that can help them get out of their situation, they would rather watch Empire than learn how to create one for their own family. When something inspires you, you must **do your own due diligence before deciding what you can or cannot do.** How would you know that your life could be changed if you won't even explore the possibilities? This book might be an inspiration and an opportunity that could change your future.

Appreciation

I want Mr. Randy and Mrs. Wanda Webb, and Mr. Ed Blunt to know how much I appreciate them. I was in another business and had no interest in looking at any other endeavors. I was totally loyal to my business, but then certain situations began to happen. I saw a video from the Webbs, and knowing they are people of true character and integrity, I became curious about what they were doing. Because I trusted them, it made a little crack in the window for me to at least check it out. A few days later, I saw another video by Mr. Ed Blunt, and I knew then that I had to investigate what they were doing. I am so glad I did!

The result of watching those two short videos has **absolutely changed my life forever.** Words cannot express what has happened to me over the past year. I just want to say to Mr. Randy and Mrs. Wanda Webb, and Mr. Ed Blunt a BIG, BIG, thank you for the inspiration. It has steered me in a new direction. I never knew Forex/Crypto existed, and my family's lives have been changed forever, for generations to come, because of you.

Table of Contents

Dedication

Inspiration

Appreciation

Foreword

Setting the Stage

Introduction

1. **It's All About Mindset**
   Meet Mr. Khalil & Nigel Stinson

2. **The History of Forex/Crypto**
   What is Forex?
   What is Crypto?

3. **What Is A Pip?**
   Meet Mr. Adrian Hummel

4. **What Is Candlestick?**

5. **What Is Support and Resistance?**
   Trend line
   Meet Mr. Julio Castaneda

6. **What Is an Indicator?**

7. **What Is A Broker?**
   What is Leverage?
   Meet Mrs. Ashjia Wraggs-Pettis

8. **What Is Risk Management?**

9. **Teach Them Young**
   Meet Mr. CJ Randolph

10. **Setting Goals**

11. **Forex Quotes**
    Meet Mr. Cory Huddleston.

12. **Final Thoughts**

Basic Definitions

Disclaimer and Terms of Use

Foreword

My background was formally known as a successful fitness entrepreneur.

A good friend of mine from college introduced me to a young man that learned Forex in such a way that he turned $200 into a $30,000 profit in less than an hour. This was very intriguing to me and it got me thrilled to learn more about the Forex. This led me to learning a skill no one can take away. I turned $500 into over seven figures in less than twelve months. Now, I'm a Forex educator, and a mentor of over a couple hundred people. This also led me into launching my own capital management firm.

All my life I've always wanted to help people. If people will take the time to learn this skill it will positively impact their lives, just as it has done for many others.

I met Coach Randolph through his son, CJ. Not only did I become his mentor, but we became great friends over the last year.

Not to be cliché, but anything Coach Carl puts his hands on always turns into gold. He is extremely talented, and due to the fact that he's a super student, he is always looking to enhance his craft! For this fact, when he speaks don't just listen – I would also take notes!

In the book, *Learn the New Rules of Money*, you will learn the basics of Forex. It will also break down mindset, risk management, and many other important things that you would need to know to be a successful trader.

Carl "Coach" Randolph
LEARN THE NEW RULES OF MONEY

If you're looking for a better life with style, and you still have dreams and goals that you would like to accomplish, then I believe this book will highly impact you with the necessary groundwork to get started. Read it with the intentions of learning. I wish you nothing but great success along your journey of living the good life!

~**Jon Spencer**
Rhino Capital
Instagram: @Mr.jSpence

Setting the Stage

When I decided to write this book, I wanted to teach everybody how to trade Forex/Crypto. After a while I began to realize that, **in my humble opinion**, it's hard to learn how to trade Forex/Crypto from reading a book alone. It was going to require writing about 500 to 600 pages of information before I would be able to tell the complete story. Because there are so many moving parts, I am sharing some of the basic information about Forex/Crypto to help you decide whether to pursue additional knowledge and understanding about it, or not.

What typically happens in the educational life of the average American is: the most trusted person you know taking you to a building known as school and leaving you there for a scheduled number of hours, from Monday through Friday. This is a process that usually begins between the ages of four and five, as you progress from pre-kindergarten to the twelfth grade …and it goes something like this:

Pre-school and Kindergarten • Elementary School: First grade to Fifth grade • Middle School: Sixth grade to Eighth grade • High School: Ninth grade to Twelfth grade. And then, for many, it's off to college, with some going further, pursuing even higher educational degrees.

From what I have seen, nowhere - from pre-school to college – are there any courses on how to trade Forex/Crypto.

There might be some, but I couldn't find them. Nor were there any on how to become a successful trader. I've heard it said in several different ways that, on average, 85% of the people in America spend between eight and twelve hours a day at jobs they don't like, doing something that they don't enjoy. If you fit that description, hopefully your outlook will change over the next few months, or by next year.

Take a few minutes in a quiet place and ask yourself these two questions, and write your answer to each in the blank provided, where you can see it:

1. Am I where I thought I would be financially at this point in my life? _____.

2. If I continue to do what I'm doing right now, will I achieve my dreams and goals anytime soon? _____.

If you answered **"No"** to either question, then I have a third one: Are you ready and willing to devote the time necessary to learn a new skill that could possibly achieve the dreams and goals you've set? *Learn the New Rules of Money* will introduce some of the different options you have to maximize the money you earn. You can gain control of your financial future. Once you start making money, seek out others that can help you learn how to wisely invest your money in different places, and not to just put it in the bank.

After I watched Randy and Ed's videos, I jumped on YouTube and watched as many videos as I could find about Forex.

A lot of them were good, some were bad, and a few were quite impressive. I viewed some videos that were recorded by a young lady named Dr. Kathy. She shared how she had almost lost everything then started learning Forex. In eight months her **$40 investment yielded her over a million dollars.** (Please be advised that this is NOT the norm though!) I thought to myself, I would love to meet this young lady one day. Well, in July 2019 I found myself sitting in a three-hour training session she led in Houston. I ask her if she wouldn't mind adding a message in my new book, and she said, "Sure. I don't have a problem with that". This is what she said about the concept of Forex:

"Forex is a God-inspired skill set in a man-made company. It is biblically referenced in Ecclesiastes 11:1 in the Good News Translation. It says that it is good to enter into foreign trade because you never know what bad luck this world is going to give you. And if Solomon - the richest man in the Bible and the wisest one that ever lived, that God said after him there will be no other - if he said that it was good to enter into foreign trade and that you should have seven streams of income just to survive, the way that you do it is not by working seven or eight jobs. You do it by trading foreign currency".

Whether you believe in the Bible or not, today there are a lot of believers and non-believers trading Forex …and making money. At the end of chapter 11, you will read Cory's story. He learned how to trade Forex while serving a 20 year federal prison sentence. Because of the **technology and apps** that we have available today, you can learn how to trade Forex from your smart phone. Imagine that - **making money right from your cell.**

Introduction

Let me temper your expectations right up front. You will not be an expert trader by the time you finish reading this book. Odds are you will not be able to go out and start trading on a live account and win big. As a matter of fact, you probably won't be able start trading live at all. However, once you find a teacher, mentor or someone that has traveled the Forex road to help you, you will be far more advanced than the person that hasn't read this book. The reason I say that is, **I truly don't believe the average person can learn the art of trading live just by reading a book** because there are too many moving parts. The market moves in a pattern. But because only a certain number of moves can be made hourly, daily, weekly, monthly or annually, without understanding what you are looking for, it will be difficult for you to just jump into trading.

To make this book as authentic as possible, I personally learned how to trade in about fifteen different styles. I researched the four major styles - scalping, intra-day, positional, and swinging. To be completely honest with you, I also blew my live account at least fifteen different times. But I learned a lesson each time and it **helped me to do actual hands-on research,** which should keep you from making the same mistakes I made. I wanted to share some of the things I personally witnessed and experienced, not just what I've heard other people say. Experience supersedes knowledge. Although my goal was to write in the simplest way I could, reading it may be like learning a foreign language because there are a lot of words and jargon that are specific to the

Forex market. Over the years of dealing with many people, and interviewing some of them, I have come to the conclusion that most of us want the same things in life: to be happy, have money, travel, take care of our family, etc. With that being said, I have also learned that you will never be able to work out somebody else's problem. Although you can offer help, each person must master his or her own individual situation. Take the time to study and learn this skill, because nobody else can do it for you.

The information in the following pages will probably not make much sense to you in the beginning, but it will come together in time. Just like a baby taking its first steps, there are many falls before they learn how to walk. Forex/Crypto is no different. It will take a little time to learn it, understand it, and to read and analyze the direction of the market. It is crucial to take notes as you read, so you can refer back to them later. Like my two other books, *How to Make Contacts and Win Friends* and *How to Find Your Passion and Get What You Want*, this book will be interactive. The reason I do this is because the more engaged you are, adding your feelings and thoughts, the more you will remember. I want you to understand what is being presented, and to reply in your own words. The best way to do that is to write it down. At the end of a few chapters, your knowledge will be tested through a few simple questions. Take the time to answer them, as this will help you retain the information. Throughout this book I will be giving you some warnings about Forex/Crypto and the market, but at the end of this chapter there will be a reminder of the one that I consider to be the most important: No matter what you've heard or read, in my personal opinion and experience, if you think the market can be predicted by your trades, you will lose.

I say the number one warning is that **you can't predict the market,** because you don't control the market. There are certain candle patterns, certain market structures, that happen at certain times. You will get to a point where you can anticipate the market based on what you've learned and by watching certain patterns, but it can quickly move in a different direction. Because of all the obstacles and other things that you can't foresee, anticipating the direction that the market is heading does not necessarily lead to an accurate prediction. I was inspired to write this book because, as I began studying and learning how Forex/Crypto currency works, I thought to myself, this knowledge needs to be shared with more people. In my heart, I was compelled to write this book. **Forex/Crypto is so powerful** and, once learned, it is a skill that can change a family's financial future for generations to come. I believe someone in your family needs to learn this skill because, if taught in the proper way, it is an opportunity that can literally change lives. I felt in my heart and in my spirit to at least share this information with anyone willing to "listen and learn". This book will give you a strong basic overview and understanding, along with the psychology and philosophy, in the best practices for trading in the Forex/Crypto foreign currency market.

Reading this book will lead to making you a better trader, if you take the time to understand the process. However, I will always be truthful about what you can expect, and help you enhance your trading skills, with proper mentoring. The art of trading is not something you learn overnight, so I would strongly encourage doing additional research.

Seek trainers or teachers that are engaged in trading and understand how the market works. The people who understand how the market flows can guide you in the correct way to make as much money as you want, depending on your ability to learn and act on the information received. You can learn the basics of Forex/Crypto currency from YouTube videos, books, and seminars that range from $300 a day to over $2000 for a weekend. In general, most people will need a little more training than a few days, a weekend, or even a few months. I was talking to one of my son's friends and he mentioned that he paid over $30k to learn Forex.

Each person will learn at different levels, and at a different pace. It is your commitment, your willingness to listen and learn, and how serious you are about trading that will yield you a positive result. One great thing about learning to trade is that you have the option to use a demo account first. It's **"play money"**, but you will be trading in the real market, in real time. This is an amazing opportunity to test your skill first, without using your hard-earned money. I've had many people who want to get minimal training and then jump into the live market. They think they are going to make a lot of money after learning a small portion of how to trade. That's not how it works. However, if you're the person who is ready to learn a new skill that can potentially change the trajectory of your family's financial future, then read on.

Please, take heed to my warnings at the end of the even-numbered chapters, because they are there for a reason. You will also have a treat at the end of the odd-numbered chapters, where you will read the testimonies of a few people who took the time to learn this skill, and what it has done for them.

These are ordinary people, none of whom have worked on Wall Street for years making millions and millions of dollars trading. They are ordinary people doing extraordinary things because they were introduced to Forex/Crypto. Each story is true, and the actual experience of the individual.

#1. "You can't predict the market". You can learn how to anticipate the market but trying to predict the market is not a good idea.

Chapter 1

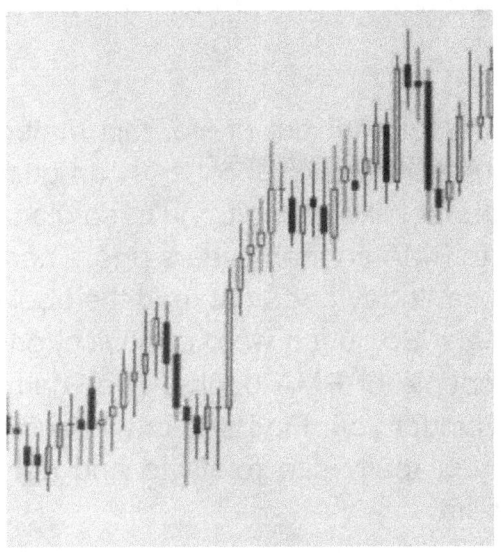

It's All About Mindset

I know you're probably saying, Coach will you just please get to the point and tell me how I can learn to trade and make all this money! If you don't have the proper mindset FIRST, it really doesn't matter how much you learn. You must approach trading with the right attitude and perspective regarding training. Whatever you do, **do not skip this chapter.** The subject is not about trading, but it will make a profound impact on your ability to trade. Positive Mental Attitude (PMA) books, CDs, DVDs, and videos can and will make a big difference in your life. The very first book I read on my journey was *Think and Grow Rich* by Napoleon Hill. I have several other favorites, which I will list at the end of this chapter. Although my book is about the basics of trading, your state of mind will also play a major part in your plan. PMA information will help you stay focused, turning away from all the distractions that will come your way.

Whatever you want out of life, this material can help you maintain a **"no quit" attitud**e. (Because I can guarantee, there will be times when you feel like giving up.) I'm so glad and grateful that I was introduced to PMA so many years ago. There is just no way I would be where I am today had I not read the books and listened to other PMA materials. So, just a word of advice, once you finish this book, pick up a couple of PMA books. They can only help you in your journey, not hinder you. Find one or two authors from the list I will provide that you really can relate to and get their material to help change your life.

I have always been a relatively positive person, although we all go through ups and downs. There was a point when life was not going my way and I found myself having to deal with a lot of negative situations. My business was tanking big time, and a lot of people did not honor what they said they would do. I had lost a significant amount of money in a real estate deal because one of the partners got greedy. It took me ten years to pay that debt. I vowed that I would never start another business again. I called a good friend who has also been a mentor to me for many years, Mr. Johnny Wimbrey, and we talked for a few minutes. He told me to come to his house. When I got there, he gave me a few books and a few packs of CDs. The value on the package was $286 but he gave them to me free of charge. I have never forgotten that.

Anyway, as I was riding home, I grabbed a CD and started listening to it. It was a CD by Les Brown, Johnny Wimbrey and Jerry Clark. Well, I can honestly tell you, that CD changed my life immensely because Les Brown said something that hit me right in my face and pierced my heart. He said, **"I wasn't playing to win, I was playing not to get hurt".** I knew, and I could feel exactly what he was talking about. That one statement opened a little crack in the window of my soul, because I had closed it off as far as dealing with people. The very next day I was at the house of another friend, Mr. Craig Sweet, and as I was leaving, he asked if I would be interested in a business opportunity to make some extra money. If I had not listened to that CD the day before, I would not have taken home the information he offered me that night. You never know how the dots will connect. In my second book, *How to Find Your Passion and Get What You Want*, I talk about connecting the dots backward. (I also have a resource page in the book with a few suggestions of other books to read. I highly encourage my readers to include *It's Not Over Until I Win* by Les Brown in their library. It is one you my favorite books, ever.)

It is so funny how the dots come back to you, full circle. Let me explain my point: Many years ago, I met a couple in church, and we became friends. One day I was at their house in the garage and from the tape player I could hear somebody talking about you have to be hungry, and I asked, "Chris, who in the heck is that?" He said it was Les Brown. I asked if I could borrow the cassette (for the younger folks that was a recorder that played sound from a little cassette tape). I didn't consider buying my own tape at that time …but anyway, I listened to that tape about ten times in a row! I was excited and ready to take on the world. I was pumped up and ready to attack life head on, no matter the repercussions.

A few years later I was fortunate enough to meet Les when he came to Dallas. It was an absolutely awesome time! I still have a picture of my best friend, Tracy Day, Mrs. Gladys Brown (Knight) and Les in my cell phone to this very day. Les has no idea the impact he has made in my life, and many other people that I know.

There are two words that can help or hurt you when trading. The first one was hard for me in the beginning, and because of the second one, I have blown a few accounts several times. You will gain a better understanding of what I mean once you start trading. In my defense though, I made some trades that I normally would not have, were I not writing this book. I wanted the information I shared to be purely my experience, not what I read.

The first word is **PATIENCE:**

Pace yourself - take time to learn and understand trading.

Attitude - you must have the right attitude when you trade.

Timing – it's all about timing; is this the right time?

Identify your style - learn which trading style suits you best.

Emotional - you must take emotion out of trading.

Never Quit Learning - have a never quit attitude and always be in a learning mode.

Calm or Cool - when you are confident with your skills, be calm while you trade.

Evidence - as you grow and start making money, you will have the evidence that trading works.

When not to trade:

I would highly encourage you not to trade when you have personal problems that are distracting; when you have a substantial financial struggle; when you're stressed out; when you are just not feeling confident on that day; or when you've had a disagreement with someone. Any one of these scenarios will make it difficult to trade because you may do things that you would not normally do, based on your state of mind. I would suggest determining ways to calm and relax yourself BEFORE starting to trade. (Make a list for future reference,) I will discuss this a little more in-depth in the Setting Goals chapter.

When you break it down, trading is a fairly simple formula and method that you will learn in your own way. One of the biggest challenges I see is when you try to force a trade, I would highly suggest doing a few things before you even start your trade day. I like listening to relaxing music or drinking my favor beverage, to relax my mind. Learn how to get into a calm state of mind because you want to **take the emotions out of trading.** There are going to be some days where you will need to just put your trades down and come back in a day or so.

The second word is **GREED:**

Get proper training.

Rebelling against your trainer, teacher or mentor is not advised.

Eagerness can lead to live trading too early.

Expectations too high leads to overleveraging and not using proper risk management.

Doomed to fail, if you are too greedy and not willing to learn the right way.

Those two words, patience and greed, are very personal to me because I had to learn each the hard way. However, they have served me well, now that I understand why it is so important to master them both. You may have heard that patience is a virtue, but in trading, **patience is a must.** There are a lot of things a mentor or teacher can teach, but there are two things that cannot be taught - patience and discipline.

Question:

Can you think back and connect some of the dots in your life?

This is an example:

1. Went to high school with Tracy and became good friends.
2. Tracy helped me get a job at the post office.
3. I was transferred to the post office on the other side of town.
4. I met a young lady working in the building next to the post office.
5. We started talking, and then dating.
6. We got married and she is the love of my life.
7. We have two beautiful children that bring me joy every day.

Write down a few connections in your life that brought you to today. As you are writing, think about what would have happened if just one of those connections did not occur.

Notes: _____
_____
_____
_____
_____
_____
_____
_____
_____
_____
_____
_____
_____
_____
_____
_____
_____

Meet Mr. Khalil & Nigel Stinton

My twin brother Khalil and I have always been close, and we talked about all the things we would accomplish in our childhood; from the girls we would date, house we would live in, and the things we would invent! We always knew we would be successful, but we just didn't know what that would be or entail. This mentality came from growing up in an entrepreneurial environment, thanks to our Mom and Dad, who have been in business for themselves all our life. They showed us that we could do anything if we set our mind to it.

Right after graduating high school we got jobs at Chick-Fil-A, which was the start to our entrepreneurial journey. Chick-Fil-A set the standard and raised the bar for customer service. We learned that if you go above and beyond and do more than you are asked, eventually you will get paid for more than you do.

Although working taught us a lot, there was one day where this feeling of repetitiveness overwhelmed us. On a Tuesday afternoon, an older lady, who had to be in her early 60s, walked in the door for an interview to work with us. Time started to slow down at that moment. While everyone else thought this was normal, my brother and I looked at each other with complete shock: "What did she do in her life that led her here?"; "She is my grandma's age and shouldn't be working anymore"; and "Does anybody else see what's wrong here?", was what we thought in our heads. From that moment, we realized that we would rather work 24/7 for ourselves than hourly for somebody else.

A friend of ours, that we had just started to get to know, who was successful in the business he was in, left to pursue something else. One day my brother saw on his Snapchat story that he was posting charts that were on his computer and somehow the skill set of being able to read these charts made him money. My brother met up with him later that day and the rest is history. Fast forward a few years later, and at the age of 22 years old we have been able to travel the world, give money to our parents, and literally impact thousands of lives. We could have been closed-minded to the idea and allowed the skepticism to keep us from learning more about Forex. The biggest risk in life is not taking one at all; what did we have to lose? This wasn't a life or death scenario. What did it cost? We didn't look at what it would cost to get into investing, we looked at what would it have cost us by not getting involved. What did we gain? Everything plus more. We used to get paid $9 an hour, and now we have been able to make six figure incomes, so you tell us.

It's simple: you don't have to be great to start; you just have to start to be great!

Khalil & Nigel Stinson
Nigel Instagram @NigelStinson
Khalil Instagram @khalil.Stinson

PMA book resources:

Life Without Limits by Nick Vujicic

It's Not Over Until You Win by Les Brown

How to Find Your Passion and Get What You Want by Carl Randolph

Rich Dad Poor Dad by Robert Kiyosaki

The Secret to Success: When You Want to Succeed as Bad as You Want to Breathe by Eric Thomas

From the Hood to Doing Good by Johnny Wimbrey

Dare to Be a Difference Maker (Vol 4) Ziglar Legacy (Tracy Day)

The Power of I Am by Joel Osteen

Think and Grow Rich by Napoleon Hill

As A Man Thinketh by James Allen

Awaken the Giant Within by Anthony Robbins

The Magic of Thinking Big By David J. Schwartz, Ph.D.

Let it Go by T.D. Jakes

There are so many more books I could recommend, but most of the authors listed have other materials you can access. Go to YouTube and research to see which ones you like, and then fill your spirit with their information.

Chapter 2

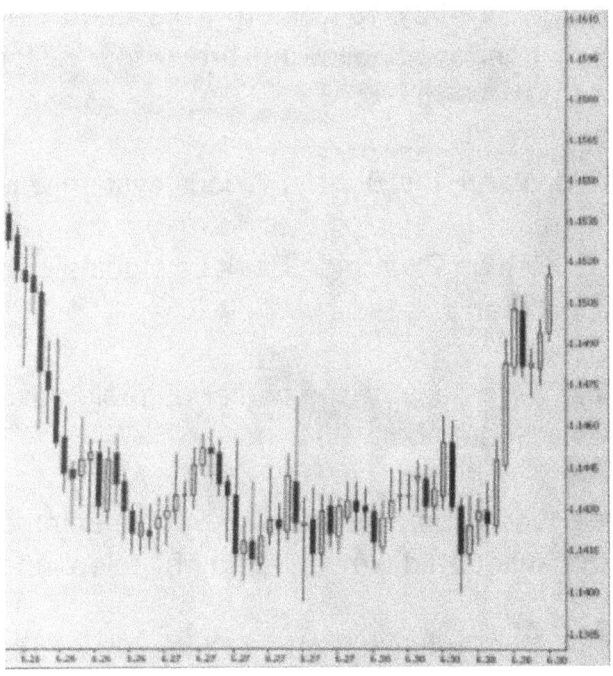

The History of Forex/Crypto

Trading currency started thousands of years ago, but it was called bartering back then. You would exchange one item or service for another. However, trading currency has evolved over the centuries and we now call it foreign exchange, or Forex. Egyptians and Greeks started trading goods and currencies about 2500 years ago. They used molten gold and silver coins. The weight and size of the coin determined the value. About a thousand years ago, copper was used more and brought down the value of the currency. Many years later, a government monopoly started when the Roman Empire established centralized currency minting. The world's oldest bank, Monte dei Paschi, was created in Italy to help with currency transactions. The first Forex market was created years later in Amsterdam, and by 1913 there were about seventy trading firms created in London. Following are a few historical facts to enjoy:

A. During World War II, the Bretton Woods system was introduced.

B. In 1954, the Foreign Exchange Bank Law guidelines were introduced in Japan.

C. The Bank of Tokyo became the center of foreign exchange approximately September 1954.

D. Reuters introduced computer monitors in the summer of 1973, replacing the antiquated way of trading by telephone and telex.

E. January 1981, the People's Bank of China allowed certain domestic "enterprises" to participate in foreign exchange trading.

F. The South Korean government allowed free trade to occur for the first time, ending Forex controls in 1981.

G. In 1981, Iran changed international agreements with some countries from oil-barter to foreign exchange.

Today, there are four major trading sessions around the world that operate 24 hours a day, Monday through Friday, and 24 hours a day, seven days a week with crypto currency, allowing access to trade anytime. Forex is the largest financial market worldwide, trading over **$5.3 trillion daily.** These are the four major sessions:

1. *London from 3 a.m. to 12 p.m. EST.*
2. *New York from 8 a.m. to 5 p.m. EST.*
3. *Asian from 5 p.m. to 2 a.m. EST.*
4. *Tokyo from 7 p.m. to 4 a.m. EST.*

The following session times overlap**:**

London and New York: between 8 a.m. — 12 p.m. EST
Asian and Tokyo: between 7 p.m. — 2 a.m. EST
Tokyo and London: between 3 a.m. — 4 a.m. EST

Of the four sessions, London is the largest, yielding high volumes of trade. There is not a clearing house or central exchange for the Forex market. The market is negotiated directly between the broker and the dealer, and foreign exchange is traded over-the-counter.

You will be trading against some of the larger businesses and institutions in the world, including:

Retail Traders
Investors and Institutions
Banks
Companies and Businesses
Central Banks

A few of the major banks that trade in the Forex financial market:

United States Citi
United States JP Morgan Switzerland UBS
Germany Deutsche Bank
United States Bank of America Merrill Lynch
United Kingdom Barclays
United States Goldman Sachs United Kingdom HSBC
United Kingdom XTX Markets
United States Morgan Stanley

You will also be competing against other traders, so **learning this skill the correct way is vital to your success.** Trading volume has increased rapidly over time because, in the last hundred years, the foreign exchange has undergone some dramatic transformations. The Bretton Woods Agreement, set up in 1944, remained intact until the early 1970s. (Your research can start by reading about the agreement!)

What is Forex?

I can explain Forex better by telling a story. Dirk and Stacie planned a trip to London, because Stacie always wanted to see the London Bridge and ride on the London Eye. Once in London, they had to find a currency exchange booth at the airport or a bank to convert their U.S. dollars into British pounds. They had a lot of fun and, along with their two sons, Dirk and Stacie were able to enjoy the sights. Before the trip back home, they had to exchange the remaining pounds back to dollars. Forex is exchanging one currency for another. Let's say you find yourself in Japan and see on the display screen at the currency exchange counter that your one dollar is equal to one hundred yen. You may think, I'm going to be rich after I exchange all my money! However, after you shop and pick up a few items, you find out that one hundred yen does not go very far. That's Forex - you sold dollars and bought yen. You are participating in the Forex market anytime you exchange one currency for another.

The most basic definition of currency trading is the act of buying and selling different currencies of the world. If you are ever at the currency counter, there will be a screen displaying exchange rates for different currency, with codes like USD and ZAR. Currency is abbreviated by using symbols (USD, CAD etc). There are many currencies that are traded every day but a few of the major currencies include:

A. (USD) U.S. Dollar
B. (EUR) European Euro
C. (JPY) Japanese Yen
D. (GBP) British Pound
E. (CHF) Swiss Franc or Swissy
F. (CAD) Canadian Dollar
G. (AUD) Australian Dollar or Aussie
H. (NZD) New Zealand Dollar Kiwi
I. (ZAR) South African Rand

Forex is like learning a foreign language. Once you learn it though, your conversation with other traders will evolve. The basic concept behind the Forex market is for trading currencies, one pair against another. The base currency is the first currency symbol of a currency pair, and the second currency in the pair is the counter currency.

The opposite is true when selling a currency pair. Depending on which part of the currency pair is bought or sold, either scenario can generate a profit. The Forex market is operated in the United States, Europe, and Asia with overlapping shifts, so currencies are being constantly traded, up to 24 hours a day if you include crypto. Various factors, including changes in political leadership, economic booms or busts, and even natural disasters can determine the price of each currency within the pair. Sample pairings are represented below:

- GBP/USD
- USD/CHF
- EUR/USD
- USD/JPY

Each currency pair is on its own side of the rope, like tug-of-war. Imagine each pair constantly going back and forth, with the exchange rates fluctuating based on which currency is strongest at that moment. Your job will be to learn the skill of determining the action of the pairs, to make the maximum profit.

What is Crypto?

Digital crypto currency is commonly known simply as crypto. From 2009 until today, there have been many new crypto currencies created, with more being added each year. There had been many attempts to create digital money, but most failed. However, Bitcoin, the new electronic cash system, was announced in January of 2009 by Satoshi Nakamoto. Satoshi's goal was to invent something in the digital market that would develop a Peer-to-Peer Electronic Cash System. The most important part of his invention is that he found a way to build a decentralized digital cash system. Basically, crypto is a series of numbers formulated in a way to create a value of currency used to buy or sell goods. The use of digital crypto currency is on the rise.

Most people think Bitcoin is the only crypto coin but there are many more in the marketplace. A few of the most popular ones, beside Bitcoin, are:

Ethereum (ETH)
Litcoin (LTC)
Ripple (XRP)
Dash (DASH)
Tron (TRX)
Monero (XMR)
Zcash (ZEC)
Peercoin (PPC)
Neo (NEO)
Verge (XVG)

Today, crypto currencies have become a global phenomenon but are still not understood by most people. If you are one of those that don't understand, don't worry. Some banks, governments and many companies are still not aware of the full impact crypto will have in the future. Crypto is here, and I believe it is here to stay. Due to ongoing global uncertainties and seemingly unstable monetary systems, Bitcoin has become very popular in recent years. Since crypto represents an alternative to centralized and politically controlled currency forms, this type of currency may have a bright future. In my opinion, the use of digital crypto currency will only become more widespread when some of the major companies begin using it.

Crypto, like other major pairs, has a value via the exchange rate, and has symbols. Reduced to a simple definition, crypto currency is limited entries into a database that cannot be altered without fulfilling specific conditions. It can be compared to your money in a bank account having a type of verified entry into a database that validates that it is yours, and without a transaction you can't access it.

Although this book is about Forex currency pairs, a lot of traders also trade indices which are trading in the major stock exchanges. Some of the popular ones are:

FTSE 100 - trading on the London Stock Exchange and tracks the top 100 stocks. Many FTSE 100 companies are globally focused, although UK-based.

CAC 40 - CAC 40 consists of the top 40 companies listed on the Euronext Paris exchange. Index for the French stock market.

Hang Seng - 50 largest companies by market capitalization on the Hong Kong stock market. Also linked to the Chinese economy, and the wider Asian market.

Dow Jones Industrial Average - Also known as the US30. Tracks the price of the 30 largest publicly traded US companies.

Nikkei 225 - Consists of 225 top-rated companies from the Tokyo Stock Exchange. It includes prominent Japanese brands such as Toyota and Panasonic.

S&P 500 - 500 largest US stocks, representing around 80% of total US market capitalization.

DAX 30 - 30 major German companies trading on the Frankfurt Stock Exchange.

EURO STOXX 50 - 50 largest blue-chip companies in the Eurozone.

ASX 200 - The top 200 stocks on the Australian Securities Exchange.

 **# 2. Be careful not to overleverage your account.**

I would like to do a short exercise. In the Goal 1 space, begin writing down all the things you want in the next five years. Whatever comes to mind, just jot it down - new car, new home, money in the bank, college tuition paid, pay off all your bills, help your parents with expenses, give to your favorite charity, send your kids to private school or just to have extra money at the end of the month. Anything you want.

Goal 1:

Notes: _____
_____
_____
_____
_____
_____
_____
_____
_____
_____
_____
_____
_____
_____
_____
_____
_____
_____
_____

Then, in the Goal 2 space, write three of the top goals you really would like to achieve within the next year.

Goal 2:

Notes:

Now ask yourself if you can accomplish the three things you wrote down with what you are doing now? **If the answer is "no", keep reading.** Do your own due diligence to find out if Forex can help you reach those goals.

Chapter 3

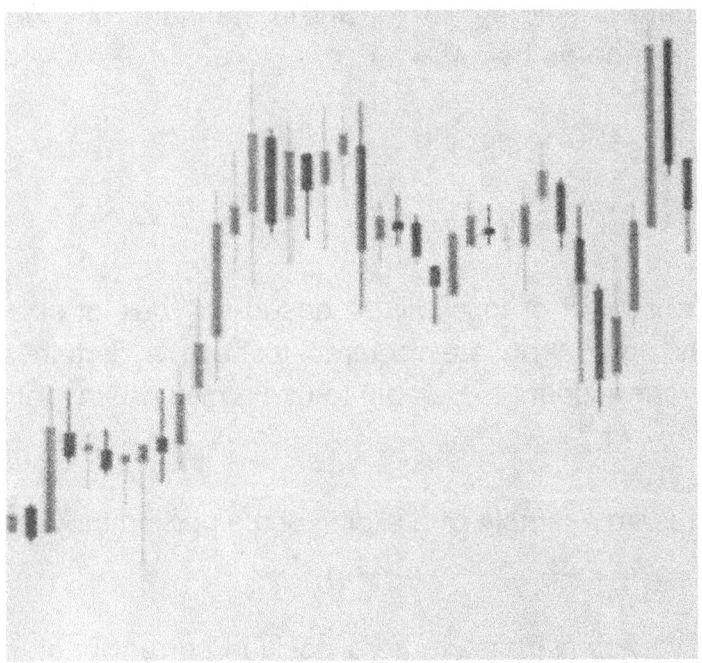

What Is a Pip?

In the trading world a pip or "Point in Percentage" is what the Forex community would consider a "point", used in calculating profits and losses. If you're ever going to be successful in trading, you will have to understand what a pip is and how they work.

There are three primary trade sizes and the average person is probably going to use the first one called a micro lot, which is the smallest size.

There is also a mini lot and a standard lot. The value of each size is denoted below:

Micro lot - .01 = $0.10 per pip
Mini lot - .10 = $1 per pip
Standard lot - 1.0 = $10 per pip

Your profit or loss will be based on your lot size and your goal for that day. You are required to have a certain amount of money in your account to be able to use a mini or standard lot size.

Figure # 1 is an example of a sliding scale per pip movement.

If you start from the zero position current price on a $100 account balance, and you move up 10 pips, which is called a buy or long, you will make 10 pips of profit. Let's say your trade was at the .10 mini lot size and the market moved 10 pips. You will make a profit of $10 for that trade. There are other factors that need to be considered, like the broker spread, but that will be explained in another chapter.

For this example, you have earned a $10 profit. That's 10% growth on a single trade! Where else can you make a 10% profit in an hour? The same is true if your trade was a sell, or short, and it moved 10 pips. Please pay close attention to the next statement. If you put in a buy but the market swings in the opposite direction, to a sell, then you will lose $10 from the balance in your trading account. The same is true if you were to enter in a sell but the market swings to a buy on your trade; you will have a $10 loss.

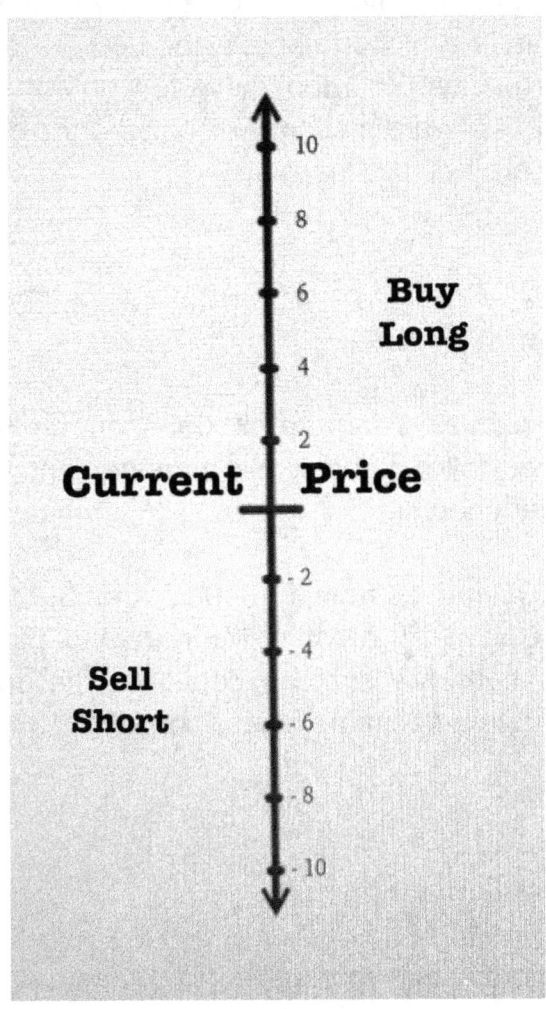

Figure # 1.

Analyzing the market is very important, before entering your trades. It may appear complicated but as you learn how to trade and get more practice, you will understand it better. When you master making a $1, all you need to do is increase the lot size to generate more money. Because each pair has a different value, it is difficult to make an overall calculation on them. You must remember that this is a global market, and you are dealing with a lot of different currencies. You don't have to worry about "doing the math" because the software platform will convert the denominations into the pairs you are trading.

What can I earn with Forex?

Earning money using Forex depends on your account balance, and if you follow proper risk management, which will be discussed in a later chapter.

If NZD/AUD moves from 1.1049 to 1.1050, that .0001 AUD rise in value is ONE PIP. Most of your trading pairs span four decimal places. There are some exceptions, like Japanese Yen pairs, which spans two decimal places. xxx/JPY 133.11 to 134.11 is one pip.

Calculating the Value of a Pip:

Each currency pair has its own relative value, and the value of a pip for that specific currency pair must be calculated.

A quote with 4 decimal places will be used in the first example.

To help explain the calculations, exchange rates will be expressed as a ratio (i.e., GBP/USD at 1.4500 will be written as "1 GBP / 1.4500 USD")

Example #1: USD/CHF = 1.0200
read as 1 USD to 1.0200 CHF (or 1 USD/1.0200 CHF)

The value change in counter currency x the exchange rate ratio = pip value (in terms of the base currency)

[.0001 CHF] x [1 USD/1.0100 CHF]

Or: [(.0001 CHF) / (1.0100 CHF)] x 1 USD = 0.00009901 USD per unit traded

Using this example, if we traded 10,000 units of USD/CHF, a one pip change to the exchange rate would be approximately a 0.99 USD change in the position value (10,000 units x 0.0000991 USD/unit). The exchange rate changes, so it is approximate because the value of each pip moves.

Example #2: EUR/JPY = 120.00 using a currency pair with the Japanese Yen as the counter currency.

The Japanese currency pair only goes to two decimal places to measure a 1 pip change in value. In this case, a one pip move would be .01 JPY.

The value change in counter currency x the exchange rate ratio = pip value (in terms of the base currency)

[.01 JPY] x [1 GBP/120.00 JPY]

Or:

[(.01 JPY) / (120.00 JPY)] x 1 EUR = 0.0000833 EUR

Although there may never be a need to use these calculations, you should have a simple understanding of how they work. As you practice and become more proficient at trading, you will get better at finding your favorites pairs and which pairs pay out better than others.

Naturally, the bigger your account size and the amount of money in it, the greater your potential earnings. If you have a daily goal to compound your effect as you trade and you grow that money over time, you can make more money faster than any bank account percentages.

So, based on your lot size per 10 pip trade, your profits would look like the ones in the list below:

.01 x 10 pips = $1.00 profit
.10 x 10 pips = $10.00 profit
1.0 x 10 pips = $100.00 profit

Meet Mr. Adrian Hummel

I've always wanted to be an investor, but I never knew how. I grew up in your average middle-class American home. My dad was a small business owner and my mom worked for the school district. I remember after college, as I started to think about my career, I became curious on how to work smarter instead of harder. At the time I was working in radio as a DJ and loved the career because I had the opportunity to connect with so many people. However, regardless of how hard I worked I never really felt I was getting ahead in life. I was working longer hours but not getting paid more. I started to get frustrated because I felt stuck.

As I started to think more and more about my situation, I began to read and educate myself on what it would take to get ahead. I began to study billionaires and tried to find clues of what they did to be successful. One thing I found is that most successful people owned assets or businesses. They were able to create products or services and, based on the market value, get paid more based on what the market would give them. To me that was interesting, however, I was reminded of how hard my dad worked and how he always seemed to be busy working in his business.

I knew there must be another way to get ahead, so I kept searching and I kept reading. I came across this book called the *Cash Flow Quadrant*, and after reading that book, it dramatically changed the way I look at money.

It made me realize that if I was going to spend my time in exchange for money, I needed to make sure that what I was spending my time on was worthwhile. That's when my wife and I went into ministry. We moved our family from Dallas to Oklahoma City and joined the staff at Life Church.

When we joined the staff, I knew that this was the best place I could spend my time and have the biggest impact. After the first year of working at the church, my daughter was born. When she was born my life changed dramatically. I felt this huge desire to make sure that she had the best options and choices in life.

I wanted her to have a better life than I did growing up, and I wanted her to live her life to the fullest potential. After she was born, I kept thinking a lot about what I learned earlier and about the cash flow quadrants. I was reminded that I needed to somehow find a way to become an investor. I didn't have very much capital at the time, and I looked at various ways to invest in real estate and businesses. I never really felt comfortable investing in real estate because you either needed to have a lot of money or take on a lot of debt. I didn't feel comfortable taking on a lot of debt, so I knew real estate, at the time, wasn't for me. I was already contributing to my 401k and started a small college fund for my daughter, but I still wanted to actively invest. I had this dream of investing in a company or a stock, getting passive income from my investments. The concept and idea seemed possible, as I had seen others do the same, so I knew it worked to some degree. But I had no idea how.

A couple years went by and I started a couple of businesses which helped increase my cash flow, but I found myself stuck working longer hours, still exchanging my time for my money. Around Christmas of 2017 a friend reached out to me about the idea and concept of Forex. When he talked to me, I had no idea what Forex was, what trading was like or how to even do a proper analysis on a chart. However, after hearing his story, I knew that this could be my chance to start investing. As I began to learn about Forex I got excited because this was something that didn't take much of my time, and once I learned the skill I'd have a way to invest and multiple my money, creating more options and possibilities for my family. I quickly became obsessed with analyzing charts and taking trades. Once I finally understood the skill and how day trading Forex works, my life started to change.

I remember when I had my first $10 day, and then my first $100 day, and before I knew it, I was having $500 days. I would show my wife and see her look in amazement at how I was able to turn $10 into $100 all from my phone. The possibilities of what Forex has given my family are endless.

We now have a way to make money, regardless of what happens in society and the world. We can spend our time and money on things we care about. I can be more present and spend more time with my family. Learning how to trade has been, by far, one of the best decisions I've made in my entire life.

Adrian Hummel
tradewithadrian@gmail.com
http://tradewithadrian.com

Chapter 4

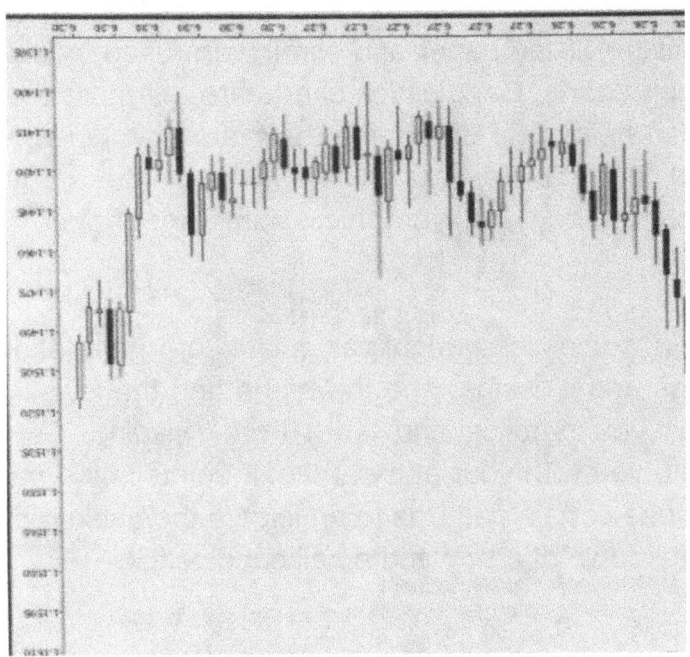

What Is a Candlestick?

When viewing a Forex chart, you will see what looks like a lot of candlesticks going upward and downward. They provide a range of information about the currency pair in the movement, helping you to develop a trading strategy.

There are several different types of charts, but the candlesticks are the most popular among traders because they are more visual. The Japanese are credited with developing the candlestick techniques. Believe it or not, the candlesticks technical charting methods were used as far back as the 1600's, giving them a rich history. Rice paper and scroll were used by the Japanese to draw their charts. Candlestick charts are the most popular, used by traders in helping to determine their strategy. Once you learn how to read the candlesticks, you will find they provide a lot of information. They are a graphical summary of price as it moves in value.

Candlesticks highlight a lot of information as far as openings and closings, and the highs and the lows, which you will learn as you practice and learn Forex trading. Candlesticks can also help you with your entry and exit points in the market. A lot of traders use certain patterns to anticipate their next move. **Figure #2** is a breakdown of a buy and a sell candlestick.

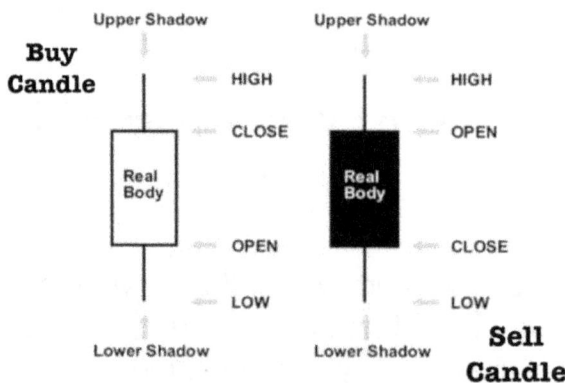

Figure # 2

The charts have different time frames - starting with 1 minute, then 5 minutes, 15 minutes, 30 minutes, 45 minutes and an hour, up to daily, weekly and monthly. Each time frame has a unique look and a different size candlestick. You may decide to choose up to two time frames, based on your trading style.

You can color code the candlesticks. Many people use green for a buy and red for a sell, while others may use blue for a buy and a dark color for a sell. It's your personal preference. If you trade on an hour time frame and see four or five green candlesticks and you drop down to a 30-minute time frame, for those four green candlesticks you will see a combination for eight to ten green and red candlesticks. Why is that? I'm glad you asked! In Forex, because the market is always moving up and down, you will see more buy and sell candlesticks on the lower time frames than on a higher time frame. Two 30 minute candlesticks equal a one-hour candlestick.

Example:

1 daily candlestick has a 24 hours candlestick.
1 hour-long candlestick have 60 one minute candlesticks.
30 minute candlesticks have two 15 minute candlesticks etc.

So, on all your trades you will need to be consistent with the time frames you choose because they add up daily, weekly, monthly and yearly. A buy candlestick (upward) is also called bullish or bull, and a sell (downward) candlestick is called bearish or bear. During the formation of a candlestick, you have the open and close price on each one based on that time frame.

Some candlesticks also have a wick at the top or bottom, and some have a wick on both ends. A wick, or shadow, shows that the bulls and the bears are fighting to take control of the market. The bulls may have had the momentum, but the bears took the momentum from them. In other words, if the candlestick was on a buy but before it closed the bears rallied with a bigger sell and then it closed, you would see a wick on that candlestick.

You don't necessarily have to use candlesticks as your price action representation. There are line charts and bar charts also.

Line Chart
A simple line chart draws a line from one closing price to the next closing price; you can see the price movement of a currency pair over a span of time, when the lines are strung together.

Bar Charts
The bar chart will show the opening and closing prices, as well as the highs and lows. The top of the bar indicates the highest price paid, while the bottom of the vertical bar indicates the lowest traded price for that time period. The horizontal hash on the right-side of the bar is the closing price, and the left-side horizontal hash is the opening price.

Exercise: Take a few minutes and answer these questions.

How many candlesticks will it take on a 5 minutes time frame to equal 1 candlestick on a 45 minutes chart? _____

How many candlesticks will it take on a 15 minutes time frame to equal 1 candlestick on a one-hour chart? _____

How many candlesticks will it take on a one-minute time frame to equal 1 candlestick on a 15 minutes chart? _____

You will use a few candlestick patterns once you start trading. There are several popular ones that traders use, with a few of the top ones listed below:

The Doji candle has zero or almost zero range between its open and close.

- Doji Star:
- Long-legged Doji
- Dragonfly Doji
- Gravestone Doji
- The Hanging Man
- The Shooting Star
- The Hammer
- Evening Star
- Morning Star

Each candlestick pattern can determine or anticipate the market direction. As you learn how to identify each candlestick, it will help with your strategy and setup. Once you learn the basics of trading you will see the importance of their role in the marketplace.

 **#3 Be mindful of the broker you choose.**

Chapter 5

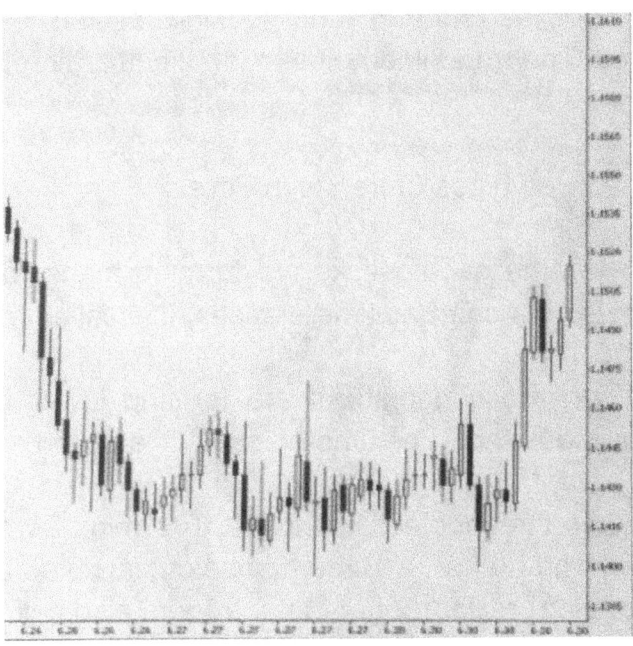

What is Support and Resistance?
Trend line

At this point, I hope that you are gaining an understanding of the Forex language. With some studying and practice, it will get easier over time.

This next subject is known as support and resistance, and trend lines. When I first heard these terms, I was so confused and just didn't **"get it"**. But over time I began to understand how important they are to a trader. The simplest way I've heard to explain the concept of support and resistance is likened to standing on the floor as support and looking at the ceiling above as resistance. The trend line helps to identify the direction of a trade.

There are three types of trends in Forex:

1. When the candlesticks are forming higher highs and higher lows on a chart as time elapses, it is called an uptrend.

2. When the candlesticks are forming lower highs and lower lows on a chart as time elapses, it is called a downtrend.

3. When the candlesticks are NOT forming lower highs or lower lows on a chart as time elapses, it is called a sideway trend, ranging, or flat range. Many traders also call it consolidation.

Support and resistance, and trend lines are the basics of trading tools. The concept of markup is something that you will definitely want to grasp and master. It is the ability to read a chart to determine price action. There are many ways that you can trade, and there are variables involved. But like everything else, you have a basic structure in trading.

Support and resistance, and trend lines are the tools you will use to become a successful trader.

Figure # 3 represents a support and resistance graph. You will want to pay particularly close attention to how many times the candlesticks hit the support or resistance lines. The more times it hits or comes close, the stronger the support or resistance. If you see several candlesticks touch a certain area and retest that area, that is considered strong support and resistance.

Once the market breaks through that specific area, whether going up, buying, or down, selling, you can determine which direction the market is moving toward. To help with that determination, you can also add a trend line. Once the candlesticks break the trend line, you can see a clear direction.

When the candlesticks, or prices, move up and then pull back, the highest point reached before it pulls back is the resistance. As the candlesticks continue up again, the lowest point reached before they climb back is the support. **Figure #4** is an example of a sell and a buy trend line.

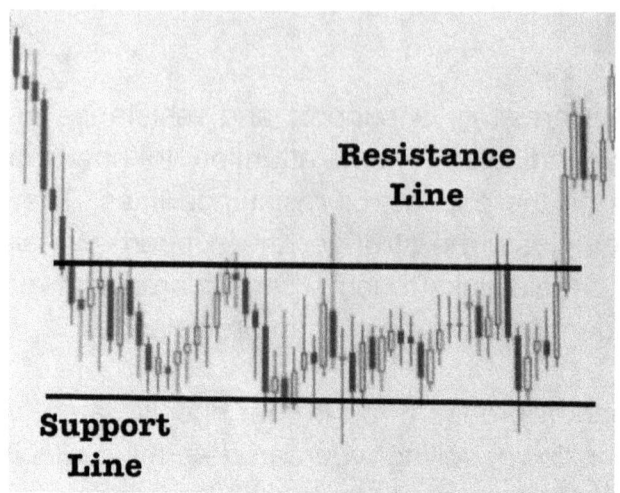

Figure # 3 - support and resistance lines

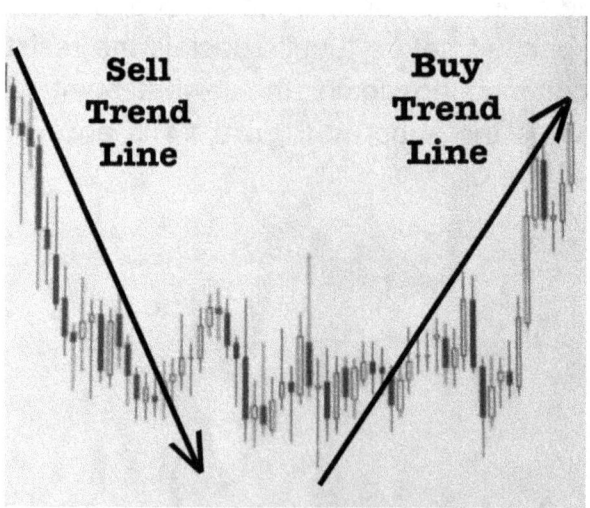

Figure # 4 - a sell and buy trend line

Meet Mr. Julio Castaneda

My name is Julio Castaneda, and I want to share a little bit of my experience in this Forex journey. I will start by letting you know where I was before Forex. I was raised in Dallas, Texas and I worked at a mechanic shop for about two years. I sold a bit of weed here and there as a side hustle (something to keep more money coming in). I wasn't happy doing either of those things. I had some money saved up, and I wanted to invest into something but wasn't sure where to start or who to ask. I looked into buying and selling cars, lawn service, breeding dogs and so many other little different ways to invest, but nothing really convinced me.

One day I was on social media, Snapchat, and I was scrolling through peoples' stories and one of my good friends, Alex, had posted a screen shot of a photo and it had two $40 profits. In the caption it read "making money off my phone", so I messaged him. I didn't get a reply, so I kept trying. After the third time, he told me he would introduce me to his mentor. We set up a meeting and I met his mentor, Jon Spencer, who is now my mentor and great friend.

Fast forward a couple of months, I put in a lot of time studying and perfecting my craft. It's almost like a sport - the more I played with it, the better I got. I went from losing all my money to gaining small amounts. Then I kept pushing, and it became a couple of hundred dollars. I'm really glad I stepped into this world. I've met so many great friends and made many connections since I started with this company. I have been able to focus more on myself health-wise. I never really had a lot of time to spend with family but now I see them more than ever. One of my future goals is to retire my parents and just be able to take care of them in every way possible. I saw them work so much and make something out of nothing. With both parents being immigrants, sometimes they had a hard time finding good paying jobs. They would work double shifts if they could, so growing up it felt normal seeing them work hard.

As I got older, I realized the struggles and exhaustion we went through. It's time to give back to the people I love and help wherever I am needed. I feel so blessed to have this opportunity to help people become financially free, because I know how it feels to come from nothing, I know how it feels to need more money than what you have, and I plan to break that chain.

Julio Castaneda
Instagram: @Julioc22
Juliocastaneda751@yahoo.com

Chapter 6

What is an Indicator?

Indicators are statistics used to measure current conditions and to forecast financial or economic trends. There are many different types of indicators in trading. Momentum indicators, volume indicators, and technical indicators are a few of them. Be very careful when choosing an indicator, make sure you base it on what you're trying to accomplish. Make sure you fully understand what that indicator does before you put in a live order. Most indicators work but you should be sure that it is built for the specific strategy you are using. You will want to conduct many, many practice trades on your demo account BEFORE you go live, especially when you are using an indicator for the first time.

When I first started trading, I had indicators all over the place. I was using seven to eight indicators at one time, and it became total confusion. You need to learn how to use one or two indicators first, based on your trading style and what you are trying to accomplish with that trade. You can use several combinations, but you want to test them as well. With any investment trade you always take a risk, but indicators can help you minimize that risk if you learn how to use them correctly. There are thousands and thousands of indicators that can help determine the direction of your trade. The market is a moving target, and **all indicators lag behind price.** Keep that in mind when you are setting up your trades. Having a coach, trainer or mentor that understands how indicators work will save you a lot of heartache, time and money. Again, most of the indicators work but the key is to use them as they are intended. Misuse can put you on the wrong side of a trade. **Figure #5** shows what a 5 and 13 exponential moving average looks like on a chart.

These are a few of the most used indicators:

MACD - Moving Average Convergence/Divergence
Bollinger Bands
RSI - Relative Strength Index
MA - Moving Average (Figure # 5)
EMA - Exponential Moving Average
SMA - Smoothed Moving Average

OBV - On Balance Volume
Mom – Momentum MF & Money Flow

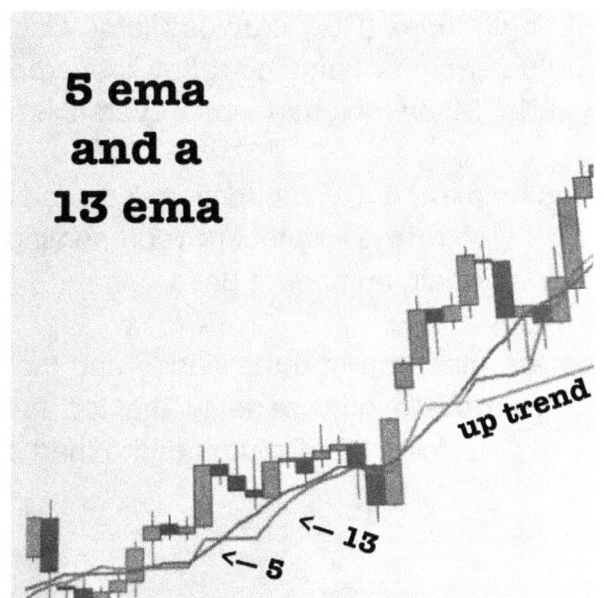

Figure # 5 shows a 5 and a 13 EMA indicator

I've heard over and over that the trend is your friend. As a new trader, it is possible to make money using a countertrend, which simply means going against the trend. However, for most traders the better approach is to recognize the direction of the major trend and attempt to profit by trading in that direction. Support and resistance, and trend line plus indicator can help.

What do some of these indicators do?

Moving Average Convergence/Divergence (MACD) is designed to gauge momentum and identify a trend. When the line crosses above the signal line, it is a buy signal. When it crosses below the signal line, it is a sell signal.

The Relative Strength Index (RSI) is an oscillator. Oscillators like the RSI help you determine when a currency is overbought above 70 or oversold under 30 on the chart, so a reversal is likely.

Moving Averages help traders with direction. You can set them to 5, 13, 50, 200 or 800, with these numbers representing the average closing price over a certain number of days.

Bollinger Bands are made up of three bands and the candlesticks, usually moving from the middle band to the top band or bottom band, helping you determine the direction of the market.

Forex Warning # 4. I would advise you not to trade on the first Friday of each month, because of non-farm payroll (NFP).

Fill is the blanks.

The trend is your _____.

All indicators _____.

Misuse of an _____ can put you on the wrong side of a trade.

Two types of indicators are _____ and _____.

Chapter 7

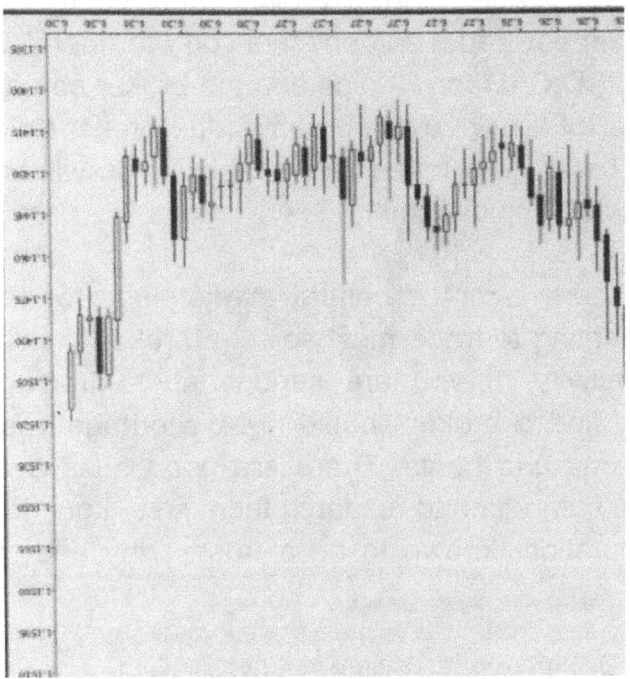

What is a Broker?

A broker, sometimes referred to as a dealer, is your lifeline to the market. Without a broker, the average person would not be able to even gain access to trade, simply because it normally requires a lot of money to get into the Forex market. We need to be grateful for the brokers because of the leverage they can provide.

However, you will need to be careful, because all brokers are not equal. People have an opportunity to participate in the

Forex market, with the broker leveraging the deals by buying and selling our trades for us. Brokers get paid a spread or commission, up front, per trade. Some brokers may charge a spread PLUS commission per trade, so don't feel sorry for them! If you are going to trade USD/CAD for 10 pips and the broker spread is 2 pips, and you use a lot size of .01 (10 cents), the broker will make 20 cents up front, before you make your 10 pips. You will have to make 12 pips to make 10 pips profit.

There is not a central marketplace for Forex/Crypto, so people wanting to trade must select a broker to help them conduct trading activity. If you are serious about trading Forex/Crypto, having to find a broker should not discourage you from pursuing your dreams and goals. There are good ones available, but you must take some time to research them first. Look for brokers with a good reputation, known to be a trustworthy and reliable financial partner.

Because of all the possibilities, you will want some basic questions answered first.

What type of customer services do they have?
How are commissions calculated?
What type of spread points are used?
How do I deposit money into my account, what are the options?
How do I retrieve my money?
Are you a regulated broker?
What is your leverage amount?
Are there different types of accounts?
What are your margins?
What currency pairs do you offer?
What is the swap commission?

From the list above, one major question that you need to ask is if the broker regulated or not? It can make a difference. There are certain laws a regulated broker must abide by that an unregulated broker doesn't have to follow. It's not my place to tell you what broker to choose. I just wanted to provide helpful information to assist, as you research further.

What is Leverage?

Once you have access to the broker's account, leverage is offered to your account. What that means is that you open an account with a small deposit, but you can control a much larger total contract value. Leverage gives you the ability to make profits, and at the same time keep risk capital to a minimum. For example, if your broker offered you a 50-to-1 leverage when you opened your account, you would have a dollar margin that would enable you to trade currencies that are worth $2,500, with a $50 deposit. What this ratio means is, for every $1 you put into your account, you can purchase up to $50 worth of currencies.

Keep in mind that leverage can also hurt you, without proper risk management. Some brokers offer higher margins and leverage, from 50-to-1 up to 200-to-1; almost like a loan. Demo, demo, and I say again, demo! **Please don't do what I did**. I only used my demo account for a week before I went live, and that was a HUGE mistake. Some of you will not listen to me, but it can potentially save you a lot of time and money if you master using your demo account before going live. My wife thought I was crazy. She would say "Baby use your demo account!". But, to my own defense, I was also testing trades I would have probably never tried were I not writing this book. I had to feel the emotion on the live account to be able to write from my heart, and the total experience.

Remember, **your demo account is FREE** and just like a live account, only with **"play money".** You are live in the market but the money in your demo account has no value. However, if you practice, practice, and then practice a little more, once you go live, watch out! You will still need to study and learn along the way though. Once you are live, you will have confidence when you trade, especially if you have a mentor, teacher or trainer guiding you along the way. We all learn by different methods, and at a different pace. You are not in competition with anyone except the person in the mirror. Just think about it, you have **NO RISK trading on a demo account,** while you learn how to navigate the market. It will be hard for some people to not go live ASAP and try to make a lot of money in a month or so. I can't control anyone else. All I can do is offer my advice. I will be the first one to admit Forex/Crypto has taught me PATIENCE.

Meet Mrs. Ashija Wraggs-Pettis

It was summer 2017 and my prayers had been answered. For almost one year, my soul had been yearning for financial strategies and wisdom. I was in the cosmetology industry for 10 years with no real retirement plan, but I had a desire to become financially free.

Well, my soul must have cried loud enough because I vividly remember that summer day; it was a Monday and I was planning to run my typical errands and then end at the library to read a book. I was not sure what book, but definitely a self-help book. Of course, all kinds of distractions came my way, but that did not stop my determination to sit down and read. I fiddled through my Kindle app and something about the title, *Cash Flow Quadrant* by Robert Kyosaki, caught my attention. I immediately purchased it and began to read.

The book was so profound in the first few pages, it only took me two days to complete. It changed the trajectory of my life by enlightening me on skills of the real estate market and the stock/forex market. I felt I was no longer walking in this world blind and I could see the light at the end of the tunnel. Divinely followed, a Rich Dad Poor Dad Real Estate event was scheduled to be in my city, literally a couple weeks after reading the book. My good friend called me with an opportunity to learn about stocks/forex through an educational company whose foundation was based on *Cash Flow Quadrant*. I was sold!

I spent the entire summer learning and gaining knowledge towards skills that I can now say have taught me how to achieve financial freedom.

Forex, for me, has provided a financial stress relief from worrying about accumulating wealth. It has also provided investment opportunities that most don't realize exist 24 hours a day, 7 days a week. I have also been able to create an additional stream of income by teaching what I have learned to many like-minded people. This skill set has broken a generational curse for many families around the world. The abundance of wealth that flows through this $5.7 trillion a day industry is truly liberating. In addition, the financial markets allowed me to understand global economics.

Financial world news is no longer spoken in a language that used to be foreign to me. Again, liberty in the world we live is available to us all. Forex is a fundamental, technical, and psychological skill set that will create financial freedom for you and your family.

Mrs. Ashjia Wraggs-Pettis
Creatingyourfinancialfuture.com
Info@creatingyourfinancialfuture.com

Chapter 8

What is Risk Management?

Of all the chapters in this book, **pay close attention to the one explaining Mindset, and this one.** To be honest with you, this is the area where a lot of traders make the most mistakes. I speak from personal experience on this one. I have overleveraged several accounts and, because I didn't use proper risk management, I may as well have simply handed my money over to my broker! The name of this book is *Learn the New Rules of Money*. If you are disciplined enough and learn the skill of risk management, this chapter will be very important to your success as a trader. Why? Because **you can create your own new rules of money**. You will be in control of your money. It's not the broker's money. It's not the bank's money, your mentor's money or your teacher's money. It's your money, and you will be equipped to control the movement.

You don't have to just put money in the bank, CDs, stocks bonds, mutual funds or 401Ks anymore. Now you have options. You can control your money, once you are generating money. You can open other accounts with different brokers and/or have several Forex/Crypto accounts. You have the option to have money set aside for different purposes, controlling where your money goes; wherever you want, whenever you want. You can continue to use that money to trade with, compounding it 10%, 15% or 20%, on top of your balance, versus letting it remain dormant in the bank or in a low paying account. My hope is that you would continue to seek the information that you need to create a generational legacy for your family. As I said, I had to learn this lesson the hard way, after blowing my account several times because of the lack of proper risk management. I had too big a lot size when I was trading, so I had to really learn to practice the skills necessary and **exercise discipline**.

I had to exercise patience and I had to learn not to be greedy, to become a successful trader. Practice on your demo account and dedicate the time necessary to really learn the process. Understanding this chapter, as you become a better and more profitable trader, is to understand what risk management really means. I have heard several different philosophies on how to handle risk management, but I personally stay with the one that my mentor taught me. Jon told me to never risk more than 5% of my total account at any one time. He teaches to risk from 3% to 5%, but no more than that. This philosophy has served me well because I tend to be more of a risk taker.

When thinking about risk management on your trades, the best advice I can give you is to play it safe. **The absolute best way not to blow your account** is to trade 0.01 lot size (10 cents) per every $100.00 in your account. So, if your trading account is $200.00, all your trades for a particular trading session shouldn't be more than 0.02 lot size (20 cents). If your account has $500.00 then your total trades should be no more than 0.05 lot size (50 cents).

Examples of 1%.

Account size.	Lot size:
$100	0.01
$200	0.02
$300	0.03
$400	0.04
$500	0.05
$600	0.06
$700	0.07
$800	0.08
$900	0.09
$1000	1.00

You would not want to put in too many trades at one dollar because that would overleverage your account, and if the trade goes in the opposite direction, you could possibly deplete your account.

But wait! There's a safety net called a stop loss (SL). When you are new to trading, I would highly recommend that you always use a stop loss. What a stop loss does is, if the trade goes in the opposite direction and hits your stop loss, it will take you out of that trade with minimal loss. However, you could also add a take profit (TP) to your trade, and when the price hits that mark, it will take you out of the trade with your profit. There are many different philosophies on how far you should put your stop loss per trade but let me explain what is called a risk/reward ratio.

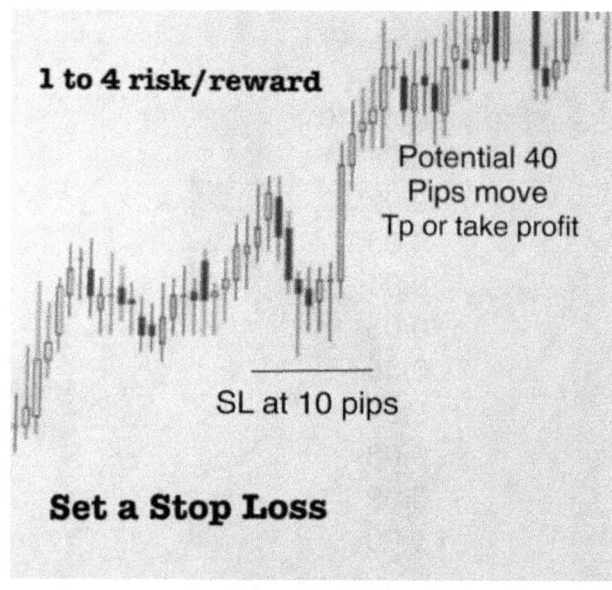

Figure # 6

You are aiming for a 40 pips profit with a 10 pip stop loss. **Figure #6** is an example of a 1-to-4 risk/reward ratio. If you have your take profit set to 20 pips and your stop loss also set to 20 pips, that is a 1-to-1 risk/reward ratio. My advice to you, if you are a big risk taker, as I am, is to learn how to discipline yourself and only trade a certain percentage of your account, setting a limit. Put it in writing and have it in front of you, before you trade for that day. Set a rule that you will not go over a specific percentage amount of your account for all your trades. You will also want to be careful when you win several trades in a row. If you're a big risk taker, you'll probably want to up your lot size to gain an even greater profit. But be very careful here. Past experiences and profits are not an accurate gauge for future profits on every trade. So, keeping your risk management in mind at all times, on each trade, is crucial.

You can trade anytime of the day or night for crypto, but with Forex, times of day or night vary from great to not so great for trading results. **In my opinion,** the following are some of the best times to trade:

1. When the London and the New York session overlaps.

2. The London sessions seems to have a lot of movement than the other three major sessions.

3. The middle of the week seems to show more movement, like on a Tuesday, Wednesday, and Thursday.

4. About 1½ hour or so after each session opens, the pairs seem to move a little better.

Some of the times I suggest that you might want to avoid trading:

1. New traders should not trade when there are major news events until after you have learned how to trade the news reports.

2. Try to be out of the market on Friday by noon because it seems to slow down for the weekend (unless you are a swing trader).

3. Holidays are typically slow trading days.

4. During major sporting events, the market seems to move slow as well (i.e., NBA Finals or the Superbowl).

The bottom line is if you have dreams and goals, I truly believe Forex/Crypto is a great way to accomplish them. The key is to not be a gambler but to learn the skill, master it, and maintain proper risk management on all your trades.

Three Types of Market Analysis:

There are three ways you can analyze and develop ideas to trade in the marketplace: Sentiment Analysis, Technical Analysis, and Fundamental Analysis. Some people say one is better than the other, but you need to know all three.

1. Sentiment analysis determines whether the market is bullish or bearish on the current or future fundamental outlooks, sometimes using media sources as a gauge.

2. Technical analysis is the study of price movement on the charts.

3. Fundamental analysis looks at how the country's economy is doing.

If you want to really become a master Forex/Crypto trader, learn how to use all three types of analysis. It can only help you to become a better trader.

To become a successful trader, there are five things you will want to give up:

1. Procrastination
2. Negative thinking
3. Excuses
4. Fear of failure
5. Negative people in your circle

Besides proper risk management, you will want to learn how to analyze the market as well. I know it seems like a lot of steps to take in but once you learn it, no one can take it away from you. **NO ONE will be able to determine how much money you can make,** because you will be in control.

In chapter 11 there are **24 Forex quotes** from people I have talked with or interviewed, but the next quote is one of my favorites, because I've done it a few times.

"It's better to miss the move than to get into the wrong move".

~Randy Webb

 **# 5. As a new trader, DO NOT trade against the trend.**

Questions:

If you were going to set a stop loss to 10 and your take profit to 40, what is your risk/reward ratio? _____.

If you were going to set a stop loss to 15 and your take profit to 15, what is your risk/reward ratio? _____.

If you were going to set a stop loss to 10 and your take profit to 50, what is your risk/reward ratio? _____.

Chapter 9

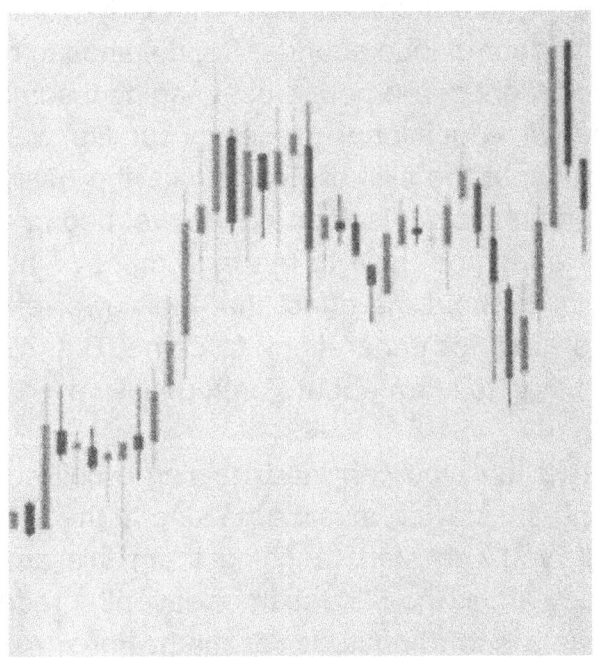

Teach Them Young

I was having a conversation with Percy Bass, a friend of my youngest son, Christian. We were discussing Forex, and during our conversation he made a statement that really gained my attention. It was about me teaching them how to trade while they are young.

Something came over me and I thought to myself, Yes! What would my life look like if I had learned Forex/Crypto when I was young? Then I told him, "Wow, that's awesome man! I am going to add a chapter to my book and subtitle it, Teach Them Young."

I've heard that a child is born with only two fears: the fear of falling and the fear of loud sounds. So, it stands to reason that all other fears are taught or learned. Just imagine if somewhere in the early fundamental educational process your life was interrupted, and you were taught the skill of Forex. Like the basics of reading, writing, and arithmetic, it is learned. If we began to teach our children, at an early age, how to manage money - how to multiply and invest it, think about the effect that the power of Forex/Crypto currency could have for generations to come. But, it's not too late for you! I didn't start to learn about Forex until I was in my sixties.

It is said that you can start training a child while they are still in the womb, by playing music or talking to them. How amazing is that? Surely you can start teaching them this amazing skill of Forex when they are in the fifth, sixth or seventh grade. If you have a child who has a strong aptitude for math, Forex may be a great skill to start teaching them now. What if you took it upon yourself to learn this skill and then, in turn, taught it to your children, nephews or nieces? What a promising future they could have. **I'm passionate about getting the word out** because I want to help change the mindset about how to generate wealth and experience financial freedom. As a matter of fact, whether you understand it or not, believe it or not, Forex/Crypto is here, and it's here to stay.

As long as we have breath there is still a chance to learn this skill, or make sure our children learn it, simply by dedicating the time.

Carl "Coach" Randolph
LEARN THE NEW RULES OF MONEY

The children are our future, so why not give them the best advantage you can, right now, knowing that there is a different way to achieve financial freedom. My oldest son, CJ, is teaching his two boys, ages six and nine, the basics of how to trade. I was in training class and the young lady teaching the class, Dr. Kathy, said she teaches eight-year old kids the art of trading. I also watched a video of Mrs. Wanda Webb teaching her children how to trade. My mentor, Jon, also teaches his son how the trade. I'm pretty sure there are many more being taught, but these are the ones I'm aware of personally. I find it to be awesome, as Percy suggested, to "teach them young". If you are a parent, I'm pretty sure you are like most parents and want your children to do better than you have. Forex/Crypto may not be the only way, but it is a great alterative for them to have under their belt. My way of thinking is not to fight it but to embrace it, learn it, study it and apply it, to help change the structure of my family situation.

People have been trading Forex for a long time and will continue to trade. Seek more knowledge, now that you have been informed. Having knowledge and doing nothing with it is just like never hearing it at all. **We owe it to the next generation to learn and pass this information on,** to help them have a better future. One of the good things about learning the Forex skill is you can build your family empire, yet never be "in the spotlight". I was talking to my friend, Arthur Guzman, and he said something that I will never forget: "Some of the more powerful people move in silence." The point being, if you are the type of person that doesn't want to be "on the front page" or getting all of the attention because of your prosperity, then Forex could be the right vehicle for you.

Meet Mr. CJ Randolph

My name is CJ Randolph. I happened to be the oldest son of the author of this book. I grew up with two younger brothers, Aaron and Christian. We were fortunate enough to have parents who always encouraged us to do and be the best we can. They always supported us in whatever we decided to do, provided it was ethical and didn't break any of God's laws.

As far as I can remember, I've always had some type of ball in my hand: soccer ball, football, basketball, etc. My love for athletics had me playing football and running track from middle school through high school, and even at the college level. I really enjoy sports, and encouraging students, which is why I became a teacher/coach. I had no intention of being an administrator or trying to be a head coach, knowing that it would limit my ability for more income unless I had a second job. Although they wanted me to be a varsity coach, the time that I would've had to spend away from my two sons, Gabriel and Gideon, was more important than the extra money as a varsity coach.

However, I was looking for alternative ways to make money and was checking into stocks, trying to figure something out. During that time, I kept running into monetary issues and just couldn't come up with the extra cash I needed. I'm so thankful to my friend, Preston, for telling me about Forex. As soon as he showed me how it worked, I was eager and ready to start learning, because I could learn on my own time at home. Also, it gives me the flexibility to have time to raise my boys with the authentic quality time they need. They want more than just me being around. They need and crave my presence.

Not only do I want to leave a foundation for my boys mentally and spiritually, but also physically and financially. I'm teaching them a skill that they can pass along to their kids, and it can't be taken away. There are many things in life that can be taken away, but wisdom is not one. It will forever live as it is passed down from generation to generation.

The funny thing about it is when I mentioned Forex to my Dad, he was actually researching how Forex worked, as well. Being able to pass it down from generation to generation just fills my heart with so much joy and happiness. As a matter fact, my Mom even got into trading. So now we have conversations, and can all understand what each other is saying, because it can sound like a foreign language at times. Now we all speak the language of legacy and we can build together as a family.

CJ Randolph
FB: CJ Randolph
Stafford, Texas

Add Extra notes you've learned so far.

Notes: _____

Notes: _____

Notes: _____

Chapter 10

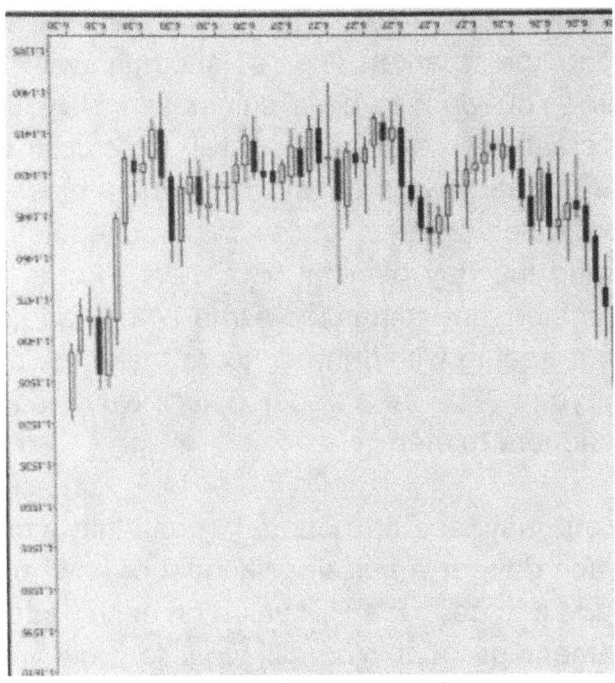

Setting Goals

You may think setting goals is not really important as part of your training but, beside your mindset and proper risk management, it will be one of the most important things you're going to have to learn.

Because the market is so vast and there are so many variables, there are many ways you can trade. You will have to set a goal and set up some rules, and then **follow them consistently to be able to become a good trader.**

It will be hard to win trades on a consistent basis if you are shooting at the market like a shotgun with pebbles going everywhere. You want to be a sniper and hit your trading target. After you create a set of goals, it will be crucial to stick with the plan. It will be vital in your quest to become a master trader. We all have different personalities, styles, work schedules, and things that we do during the day or night. But there is one thing that we all have in common, and that is the same 24 hours in a day. What you do with your trading within those hours make the difference in how successful you will be as a trader. That's why it so important to set goals and adhere to them.

You may set a monetary goal that you would like to achieve each day, or a certain PIP goal of how many you want to acquire/trade in a day, or a PIP value on each trade. I was taught to have a percentage goal. You will want to grow your account by a certain percentage each day or trade. There are so many variations in setting goals, and they may evolve as you learn how to trade, and gain experience in the market. But what you don't want to do is enter with fly-by-night trades here and there, guessing and trying to predict the market. Trading is easy once you learn the skills and follow a trading plan. As I have talked to and learned from some of the top trainers, most have a certain routine they do before trading, each day.

This is just an example of a trading day routine, with the actions being consistent each day or week:

1. Get in the right mindset.
2. Get in a place where you're comfortable, with no distractions.
3. Play some relaxing music.
4. Drink a cup of coffee, tea or your favorite beverage.
5. Get into a space where you have time to trade.
6. Have your goals written down and in front of you to follow.

Once you achieve your money goal, your percentage goal, or your PIP goal for that day, **shut down trading and enjoy the rest of your day.** You don't have to trade all day every day. As you get more experienced at trading, you will settle down into a system that will suit your style. As stated in the introduction, there are two words that can help or hurt you when it comes to trading - patience and greed. Maybe you are discouraged with your life because things may not be the way that you'd planned; maybe in the last year you've gone backward instead forward. Trust me when I say that I can relate to this, as so many others can too. When I set a goal and reached a point where I was prepared to start trading, I created an acronym to help me to stay focused. Maybe it can help you too!

BLINDERS:

BEGIN: It's time to get started. Start today by doing something.

LEAD: Your team or family needs to see you lead. You can't wait for someone else to move, you must take the initiative.

INTENTIONAL: Be intentional in all you do, based on your goals.

NEGATIVITY: Distance yourself from any place, person, or thing that doesn't lift you up.

DMO - Daily Method Operation. What you do each day. Whatever you do each day will move you closer to or further away from what you are trying to accomplish.

EVENTS: Attend trading events, especially major events. Be in the company of motivated and successful people who are doing what you aspire to do.

RESOURCES: Books, DVDs, CDs and videos; teachers, mentors or trainers.

STAY FOCUSED: You will have ups and downs but stay focused. Obstacles are there to see how bad you want it.

⚠️ *Forex Warning* **# 6. If you are having a bad day or are not "feeling it", don't trade.**

Question:

Would you say setting a goal is important? _____.

Chapter 11

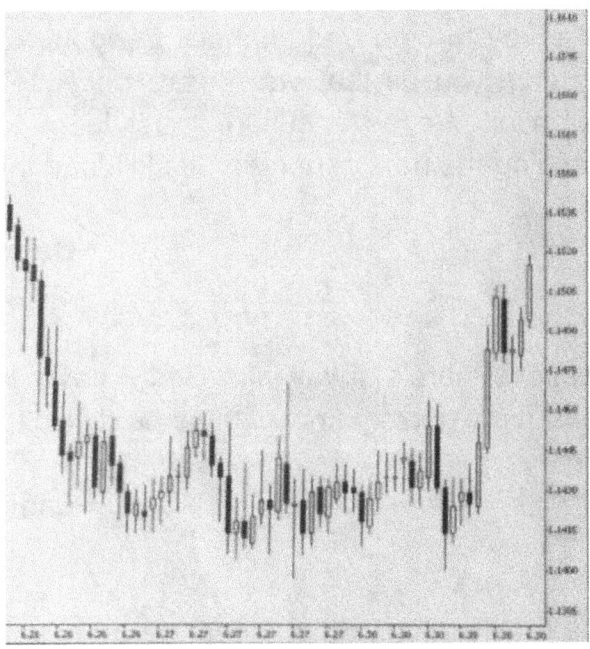

Forex Quotes

Before I give my final thoughts, I'd like you read a few Forex quotes from other people who trade.

These individuals are from different backgrounds, economic situations, and even different cultures, but the one thing they have in common is a passion for trading Forex/ Crypto.

"Forex is the key to time and financial freedom. It's a skill set that will literally give you all that you desire because of the unlimited income potential. We as a culture must learn to build a legacy through teaching the next generation a skill, and this is the best skill to teach."

~Quinn Gibson Lewis

"I always believe there's a way with God, I never lose hope or faith working toward my goals. I know it may be difficult, but I stay locked in."

~Land Shnyder Louis

"As a single mother, Forex has given me an equal opportunity with flexibility to learn a profitable skill that will forever change my family's legacy."

~Sandra Luna

"Forex has taught me to be patient and always take action despite my feelings."

~Darryl George

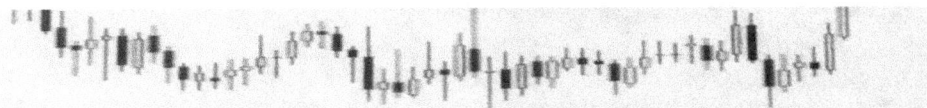

It was so exciting interviewing and talking to all these people and getting their quotes. I truly enjoy seeing people pursue their dreams and goals.

"It has given me the opportunity to provide for the people I love in more ways than one."

~**Kerven Cadet**

"Forex has given me time and freedom, allowing me to spend time with loved ones."

~**Julio Castaneda**

"Trading Forex is the only skill I've learned that has no cap on earning potential!."

~**Cory Patterson**

"I'm so thankful I found Forex because it's giving me a chance to finally reach my goals. I also get a chance to help others reach their goals, by teaching them this skill set."

~**Julio Tenezaca**

"Forex trading is not just a journey to financial wealth, it's self-discovery worth far more."

~**Shanna-Kay Britton-Edwards**

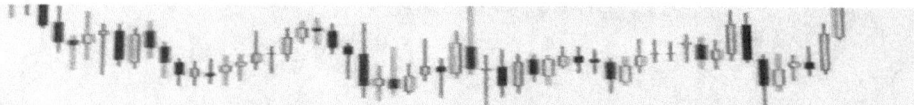

I'm a big family person and it was so refreshing to meet other people with the same mindset about taking care of their family.

"Forex for me is financial freedom, a way to have a recurring income, help others in need, and finally afford the things that I couldn't afford, and travel."

~Pauline Wong

"An opportunity to create freedom and flexibility by playing a numbers game from anywhere in the world."

~RT Adams

"If you know God called you to learn Forex, don't let anyone talk you out of what God called you to do."

~Yolanda Weston

"Forex means to me the opportunity to break the curses of financial stress and strain on my family. It breaks GENERATIONAL CURSES FOREVER."

~Regina Carson

"The opportunity and the ability to change the dynamic of my family tree, by learning a skill that will pay you forever."

~Nathan Duncan

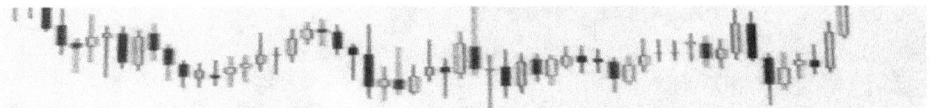

"As a single mom of three, I desired a life of freedom; freedom financially, freedom to dictate my schedule, freedom to design my perfect life. Learning the invaluable skill of trading in the foreign exchange market, Forex has afforded me the opportunity to be free."

~Dana Dimson

"Forex stretches your mindset, and once your mind is expanded it can't go back to its original financial mentality."

~Jay Smith

"Forex is the ACCESS to life that society promises degrees will give, so that you may live in EXCESS."

~Cierra E.

"Forex is my tool of choice to create endless wealth, freedom, and opportunities for those willing to endure the ups and downs of the learning process. It will be what allows me to create a dynasty for my family, free of debt and able to enjoy the beauty this world has to offer."

~Tyler Florkowski

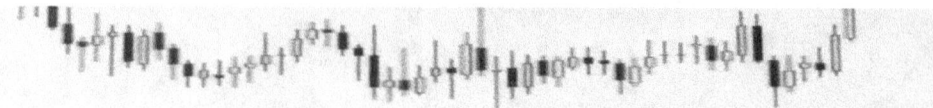

"I see where Forex will afford me the freedom to spend all the time I want to spend with my grandloves."

~Rochel Taylor

"Learning the skill of trading Forex has allowed me to earn a living from wherever I choose to live."

~Miquel Agosto

"The most amazing thing about Forex, to me, is it's a skill set that ONCE learned allows you to obtain wealth; anyone at any age can learn it and become wealthy."

~Toya "LuckieStar" Luckie

"Because of Forex, we built financial power that gives us a life many dream about. Our main goal now is leaving a legacy that teaches others how to do the same."

~ Brian and Kenya Horton

"Forex is a gateway to breaking free of that 9-5 trap."

~Kayla Dickerson

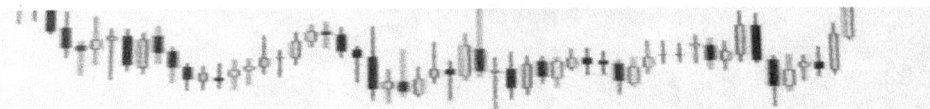

"Forex is key to my financial freedom, generational wealth, and development as an individual. Without Forex I would be lost in this world, trying to find out what I actually want to do with my life. When I found out about Forex it gave me the hope, drive, hustle, and grind that I needed to be successful in the markets. Now I'm a five figure, almost six figures trader. Thank you, FOREX for changing my life!!!!!!."

~**Don Myers**

Carl "Coach" Randolph
LEARN THE NEW RULES OF MONEY

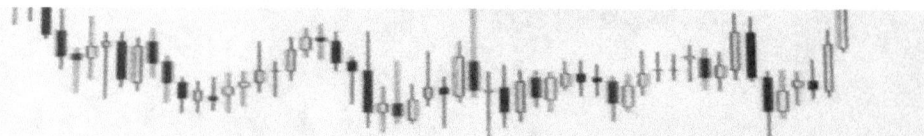

This next story is one of true redemption. It doesn't matter where you've been or what you've been through, you can always make a change in your life. Cory did, and I'm so proud of this young man. **If he can do it, despite his circumstances, you can do it too.**

Meet Mr. Cory Huddleston.

My name is Cory Huddleston, I am 41 years old, and I am from the City of St. Louis. I grew up in a household with both of my parents and four siblings. Both of my parents worked, but it was always a struggle to provide for five children. When I was old enough to work, I grabbed my first job at McDonald's, and worked there for a couple months. After McDonald's, I started job-hopping because I wanted to pursue my dream: to become a professional basketball player. That dream took a different path due to the fact that I was not offered any college scholarships to pursue a basketball career.

When I realized that becoming a professional basketball player was not going to happen at that moment, I continued to work. But there was still something in me that wasn't right. I felt that even though I was working, and this was the longest job that I had ever held in my life, I somehow felt that I was not pursuing my passion. That is when I took my last check of $160, purchased marijuana, and never looked back. This was the start of me selling drugs. Even in the midst of me selling drugs, there was an inkling inside of me that still wanted to become a professional basketball player. So I enrolled myself at St. Louis Community College-

Florissant Valley, and used my drug money to pay for school, in addition to a scholarship that was granted to me during my second semester for basketball. Even though I was enrolled in school, I was never serious about graduating and moving forward with a career. I was just there for basketball. I was too far in the drug game and was becoming comfortable with the lifestyle that I had acquired. I didn't want to let the streets go. In 2002, I caught my first case and was charged with the manufacturing and distribution of marijuana. I was sentenced to five years of probation, but I only served six months. After those six months, I was caught again, with marijuana and cocaine, and I was sentenced to eight years, but only did 120 days of shock treatment in a state prison. Six years later, not learning from my past mistakes, I was charged with possession to distribute crack cocaine and was sentenced to 20 years in a federal prison.

Before I sparked an interest in Forex, I had been incarcerated for four or five years, and during that time I was fighting to reduce my sentence. One day while I was working at my job in prison, in the commissary, a gentleman walked up to me and asked if I would be interested in attending a class about trading, and my response was "Yeah". I took the pamphlet back to my cell, started reading it, and my trading interest took off from there. I studied trading for hours for several months before I made my first trade and profit. I took $2,000 and turned that into $10,000 within six months. That is when I realized that I had discovered my passion. Trading was something that I really enjoyed doing. I started sharing my knowledge with others. I would talk about trading to anyone that would to listen, because I wanted to see them win also. They could tell that I was really passionate about trading, because, not only did it keep me occupied while fighting my time, it was something positive. Trading had become a priority for me, while my attention was focused on learning and teaching as much as I could about trading,

I received a major blessing within my 9 ½ years of being incarcerated - I received a letter from President Obama stating that my sentenced was being commuted, and I would be released within a year of receiving the letter. I was so ecstatic because I had been fighting for so long for a sentence reduction. Even though I was on my way home, I continued to grow as a Forex trader, and when I was released from prison in 2017, I took that knowledge with me and shared with family and friends, and many other individuals who were interested in learning Forex as well. I have been out of prison for two years now, and still I carry a strong desire for Forex; my desire to help others has led me to start my own signal group, which continues to grow.

This group is designed to help individuals earn as they learn, while following trading signals that I take myself as well. As a trader, not only do I want to see myself succeed, I want to see others succeed too. In today's society, it is very systematic for an individual to work a nine to five to earn income; however my dream is to teach as much as I know so others can earn money to be financially free. And, so far, my dream is working.

Cory Huddleston
HuddlestHonc989@gmail.com

Chapter 12

Final Thoughts

Throughout this book I've tried to express that you don't have to follow the traditional route of growing your money by putting it in a financial institution and making a small percentage on it. **I'm not saying not to use financial institutions;**

I'm just saying now you have other options that yield higher financial gains. If you learn Forex, and invest the money in your account, you could earn a 10%, 20% or even 30% increase on that money. But it's all based on how much you want to learn, how much you want to study, and how much you want to succeed in the Forex/Crypto currency market.

I believe in my spirit, learning Forex could **"absolutely, possibly"** be one of the best decisions you will make. It was for me and my family. All the stories in this book are true, written by the actual people. My belief is that if they can do it, you can do it too. However, it will not be an overnight, microwave skill to acquire. In my experience, it's been worth every minute I've spent learning it. I wanted the information in these pages to be as authentic as possible, so if you choose to take this path you can avoid some of the mistakes I've made. I added the warnings at the end of the even chapters for a reason. If you take heed to each of them, you will save yourself a lot of time and a lot of money. Use my experiences to assist you in becoming a better trader.

If you've reached this chapter of the book, it is obvious that you're serious about finding out how Forex/Crypto currency can help you and your family. My greatest suggestion would be to seek more information and do your own due diligence, so you can feel confident about your decision. Find someone who can help teach and guide you through all the information; a coach or mentor who can show you what Forex/Crypto currency is really all about and how it can help your financial future. More than likely, the person that referred this book to you has access to someone who can answer any questions you may have.

With the proper guidance, your **"Yes" or "No"** to learning more about Forex will be an informed choice.

In the beginning, I told you that, for the average person, it might be hard to just read a book related to trading, like this one, open a live account, and start trading that day. However, you now have a good idea about the art of trading, and a jump start on how to begin. It is completely up to you to find and dedicate the time to learn about and understand how the market works. Be careful when seeking forex training though, because you don't have to spend a lot of money to learn. I'm so glad that I decided to research how to trade the Forex/Crypto currency market. Never in my wildest dreams would I have thought we could literally make money from our cell phones. But I am grateful and so glad that we can ...and I did. It has changed my life!

I wanted to share a text I sent to Jon, who is not only my mentor but one of my trainers as well, on the day I knew I was in the right place.

"Hello Jon, just keeping you in the loop. I have been reading the telegram messages and I entered a trade on my demo account. I only used 10 cents on that trade and in 18 minutes it made $5.18. That's not very impressive, but if I had made that exact trade at $10, that would be over $500, in 18 minutes! We are getting more and more excited and are so glad we took a chance to change. I was sold already, but today I'm more than sold that anyone willing to learn this skill can make money for life".

I know in this book I've talked a lot about Forex/Crypto currency, and making money, and setting up generational wealth.

I'm not saying that money is everything, but it does have influence over just about everything in your life. **Almost every decision that you make is based on money.** Coach, what do you mean?

When you don't have money, it becomes one of your prominent thoughts. **Why?** Because it can determine where you go to eat; what kind of groceries you can buy; your choice of entertainment; what kind of car you drive, and the gas you put in it. Money determines what kind of clothes you wear, the kind of house or apartment you live in, ...you get what I'm saying. Yes, money determines just about everything you do in life.

So, if you looking for a better way and you still have dreams and goals, if you want to live a better life, contact the person that suggested this book to you for more detailed information about how you can change your future. **My prayer for writing this book is that those who read it will take action.**

When I lay my head down on the pillow each night, I have a feeling that no man, no job, no amount of money, no friends, and even no family member can give me. It is the feeling of **"PEACE"**. If the Lord took me today (but I'm not ready to go yet!), I don't have to worry about my kids or my wife, Sheryl, who is the wind beneath my wings. She and my son, CJ have also learned how to trade Forex /Crypto currency.

I might not know you but I'm so excited for you and, if you choose to learn this skill, I look forward to hearing about your trading journey one day.

I could not finish this chapter without saying a big, big, thank you to the man who worked on Wall Street, Mr. Chris Teri, and to Ms. Isis De La Torre for creating an online platform for the average person to tap into and create whatever success means to them. Because of them, plus their management team, thousands upon thousands upon thousands of people and their families will have a brighter future.

"If you will take the time to learn how to properly trade Forex and you master discipline along with patience, then I believe the only limit you have is you"

~ *Carl "Coach" Randolph*

Big Congratulations!! You are on your way to becoming a Master Trader.

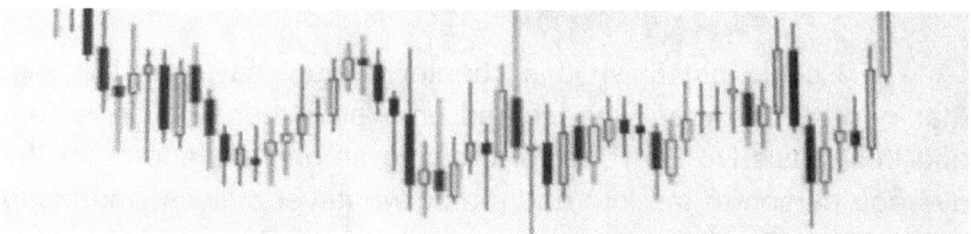

Basic Definitions.

Here are a few major definitions that are used daily in the Forex/Crypto market. There are many more, but these are some of the basic ones that are used often.

ASIAN CENTRAL BANKS: For Asian countries, refers to the central banks or monetary authorities.

BAR CHART: Financial chart with the high and low prices, tracking market movements.

BEARISH/BEAR MARKET: Negative for price direction called a sell. Example: "We are bearish GBP/USD", meaning we think the pound will weaken against the dollar.

BEARS – Traders on a sell or a short position.

BID/ASK SPREAD: The difference between your bid and the asking price.

BID PRICE: There are two prices: bid price and ask price. In FX trading, the bid represents the price at which a trader can sell the base currency; the ask is the market value.

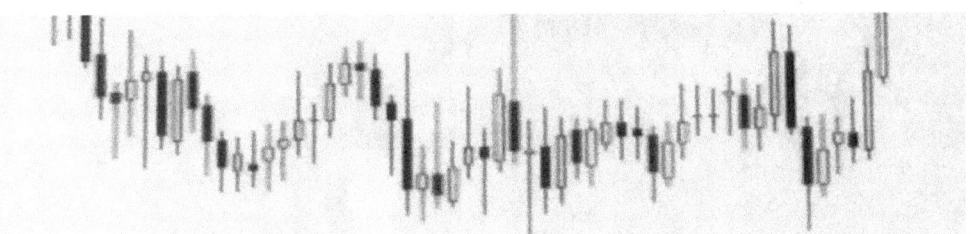

BOLLINGER BANDS: Can often indicate support and resistance levels, and plot two standard deviations on either side of a simple moving average.

BROKER: A firm that acts as an intermediary, bringing buyers and sellers together, for a fee or commission.

BULLISH/BULL MARKET: When the market is rising in prices. Also known as a buy or long position.

BULLS: Traders expecting price to rise.

BUY: Taking a long position on a product.

CAD: The Canadian dollar.

CBS: Abbreviation referring to central banks.

CANDLE STICKS: Candlestick charts are a type of financial chart for tracking market movements.

CLOSING: The process of closing, or stopping, a live trade.

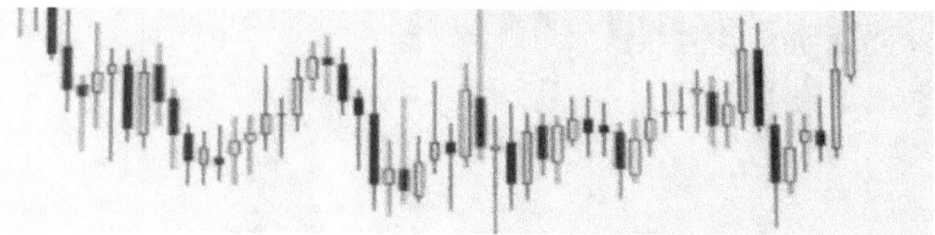

DOJI: A CURRENCY: Any form of money issued by a central bank or government and used as legal tender and a basis for trade.

candlestick formation, signifying equality and/or indecision between bulls and bears.

DOWNTREND: When price action consists of lower lows and lower highs.

ENGULFING: The Bullish/Bearish engulfing pattern is a two-candle reversal pattern. The second candle completely 'engulfs' the real body of the first one.

FUNDS: Refers to hedge fund types active in the market.

INDICATIONS: Used by traders to make decisions about market entry and exit points; calculations which take the volume and price of a certain financial instrument into account.

LEADING INDICATORS: Statistics that try to help determine the direction of the market. Indicators are usually used to forecast price changes in the market.

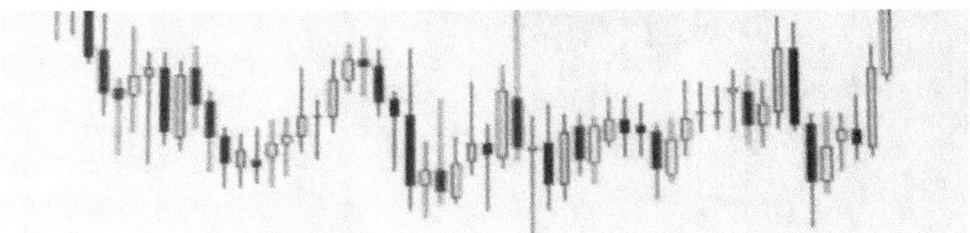

LEVERAGE: Sometimes call margin. From the amount of capital available, this is the percentage or fractional increase you can trade. It allows traders to trade notional values far higher than the capital they have.

PIPS: The smallest unit of price for any foreign currency.

PULLBACK: The market is trending in one direction but retraces back, then continue in that same direction.

RISK: The amount of money you are willing to risk on a trade.

SPREAD: The difference between the bid and offer prices.

STOP LOSS ORDER: An order placed to sell below the current price (to close a long position), or to buy above the current price (to close a short position).

SUPPORT AND RESISTANCE: Identifies price levels where, historically, the price reacted either by reversing or by slowing down; prior price behavior at these levels can leave clues for future price behavior.

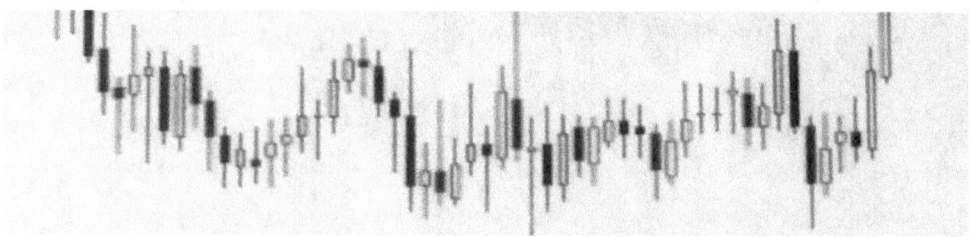

SUSPENDED TRADING: A temporary halt in the trading of a product.

TAKE PROFIT: Entering a trade, adding a take profit and, when the price hits the take profit, it will close your trade.

TREND Price: There are three ways the market moves. Up trend is identified by higher highs and higher lows. Down trend is identified by lower highs and lower lows. Sideway (consolidation) is more from side-to-side.

Disclaimer and Terms of Use

Trading in foreign exchange ("Forex or Crypto currencies") can be high risk and is not suitable for all investors. I tried my best to explain what your mindset should be before entering a trade. Past performance is not an indication of future results. Before you decide to invest in foreign exchange or crypto currencies, you should carefully assess your investment objectives, experience, and your willingness to take risks. Always keep in mind that there is a possibility that you will lose your initial investment, partially or completely. In a worst-case scenario, you should not invest any funds that you cannot afford to lose. Always keep risk management in mind on every trade. I will stress again the importance of having a successful trainer or teacher. **All the information made available here in *Learn The New Rules of Money* is provided to serve a general informational purpose only, without specific recommendations and without obligation on the publisher or the author's part.** We are not giving financial advice in any form, and do not assume the information offered as a substitute for the investment advice of a professional advisor or institution. Therefore, WE HIGHLY recommend contacting a personal financial advisor before carrying out specific transactions and investments.

Remember: **Trading currency can be risky and past results do not guarantee future results.** On all trades, do not risk more than you are willing to lose, and always use proper risk management. It's your money and your responsibility.

IF YOU'RE NOT MENTALLY PREPARED, DO NOT TRADE.

Extra Notes:

Notes:

Notes:

www.ingramcontent.com/pod-product-compliance
Lightning Source LLC
Chambersburg PA
CBHW070653220526
45466CB00001B/420